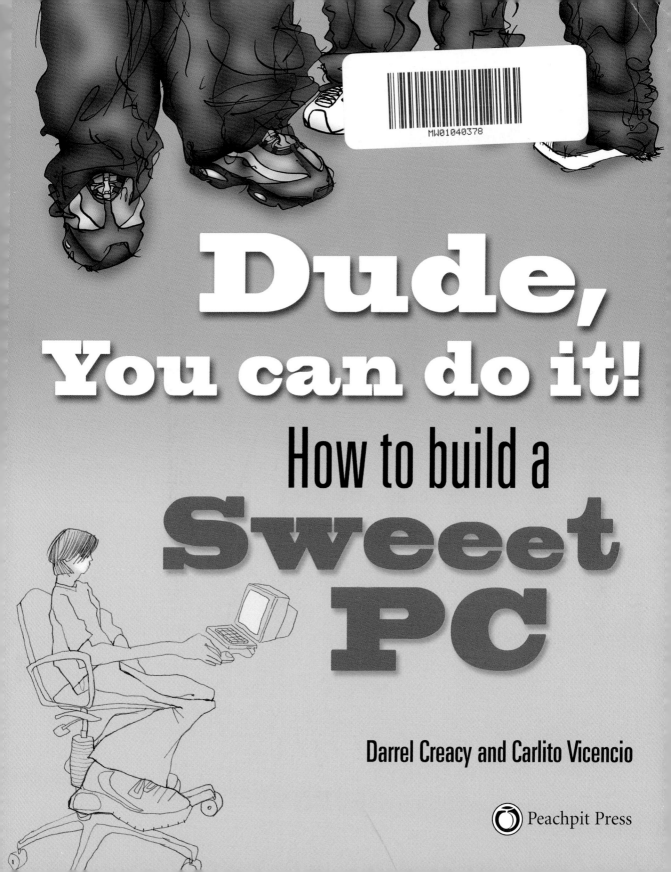

Dude,
You can do it!

How to build a

Sweeet
PC

Darrel Creacy and Carlito Vicencio

Peachpit Press

Dude, You Can Do It! How to Build a Sweeet PC
Darrel Creacy and Carlito Vicencio

Peachpit Press

1249 Eighth Street
Berkeley, CA 94710
510/524-2178
800/283-9444
510/524-2221 (fax)

Find us on the World Wide Web at: www.peachpit.com

To report errors, please send a note to errata@peachpit.com

Peachpit Press is a division of Pearson Education
Copyright © 2005 by Darrel Creacy and Carlito Vicencio
Project Editor: Cheryl England
Developmental Editor: Nikki Echler McDonald
Production Editor: Lupe Edgar
Copyeditor: Rebecca C. Rider
Compositor: Diana Van Winkle
Indexer: Karin Arrigoni
Cover design: Aren Howell
Cover illustrator: Veer
Interior design: Mimi Heft

Notice of Rights

Notice of Liability

Trademarks

ISBN 0-321-33416-7

9 8 7 6 5 4 3 2 1

Printed and bound in the United States of America

This book is dedicated to my wife Sherrie; my children Kelsie, Kyle, and Kenlie; and my parents, Carlito and Marisel. Thank you, Sherrie, for all your love and support. Kelsie, Kyle, and Kenlie, you cool kids are my inspiration. Mami y Papi, thank you for the advice and guidance. All of you believed in my many crazy ideas—this one was a success!

— Carlito

For my wonderful wife, Cheri, and our two fabulous kids, Derek and Martha. You guys are my whole world; remember that we can accomplish anything as a family and a team.

— Darrel

Table of Contents

Acknowledgements

Special thanks to all the great people at Peachpit who worked so hard on this project. Cliff and Cheryl, you believed in us, and for that we are forever grateful. Nikki, you rock. Thanks for making us do it right, babysitting us, and helping us with our kooky writing. Lupe, Rebecca, and Kim, you are a team beyond compare! Thanks for all of your hard work in making this book such a fantastic product.

We also want to express our sincere appreciation to a couple of great guys. To John Smallwood (www.smallwoodphoto.com), thanks for coming through in a pinch with style and professionalism. Your effort and experience gave this project the high quality photography it deserved. To Martin Vives, you are our good friend and talented designer. Your skills as an artist have pulled us through on many critical deadlines, thanks dude.

A Special Gift to The Women In Our Lives

We couldn't have written this book without the support of the women in our lives, too many of whom have battled breast cancer (and, thankfully, defeated it), are currently fighting the disease, or are at high risk of acquiring it. In honor of these brave ladies, we're donating 10 percent of our gross income from the sale of this book to The Breast Cancer Research Foundation.

We want to thank all of our readers for buying this book and helping to make our contribution a large and meaningful one. Every 12 minutes a woman in America dies of breast cancer, according to the National Breast Cancer Foundation (www.nationalbreastcancer.org). That woman could be your mother, your wife, or your daughter. We encourage you to visit The Breast Cancer Research Foundation's Web site at www.bcrfcure.org today and make a contribution of your own to help the women in *your* lives.

About the Authors

Darrel W. Creacy, a recently retired Coast Guard pilot who earned two United States Air Medals for heroic actions and was directly responsible for saving more than 50 lives during his search and rescue cases, began his computer building career when he met Carlito Vicencio, a newly assigned pilot to Air Station Houston.

As Darrel tells it, he had decided to buy an expensive, high-end computer that was going to set him back over three grand, but he decided against it after running the purchase past his pal, Carlito. Carlito told him to cancel the order immediately. Then he and Darrel went on to build his first computer, saving over $1,000 and building a much better PC in the process. As a result of this success, the two dudes joined forces and started Electric City Computers in December 2003.

Like peanut butter and jelly, Darrel's innate business savvy and marketing talent perfectly complemented Carlito's PC building skills. The two went on to found Dude Productions with the goal of helping the masses save money, gain usable knowledge, and break free from the Corporate Conglomerates.

Carlito R. Vicencio, a Coast Guard pilot and certified PC technician, was introduced to computers at the age of 12 when his father gave him his first Commodore 64. A hacker at heart, Carlito became fascinated with programming and went on to win several school competitions programming on the Apple IIe and the x286 computer platforms. While serving as a naval engineer in the Coast Guard—after graduating from the U.S. Coast Guard Academy with a degree in management—Carlito formed his own custom-built computer company.

Carlito met his current partner in crime when Darrel approached him about the purchase of a new PC. Not wanting to see his new friend waste money and be unsatisfied with his computer, Carlito went on to show Darrel the art of computer building, and the rest is history. With Dude Productions, Carlito and Darrel firmly believe they can start a revolution—one in which everyone can build their own computer and be free of the Big PC Vendors!

Introduction

//

A few years ago, I was just like you. Like almost every other guy in the developed world—and by developed, I mean countries where high-speed Internet access and copies of Halo 2 are readily available to anyone with a credit card and a video game addiction—I used computers for video games, work, and email, but I didn't spend much time sweating over what made them tick. I mean, I work in the Coast Guard; I'm not a computer geek. I just wanted the thing to work, right?

So when the time came for the inevitable upgrade—because it's impossible to play the latest, greatest games or edit home movies on last year's plodding processors and outdated operating systems—I went online to order my sweet PC from none other than Dell. Dude, who else? It was a sweet rig with the fastest processor money could buy and all this other fancy stuff I thought I needed.

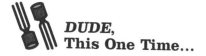

DUDE, This One Time...

I (Carlito) built my first computer eight years ago with the help of my friend Mike Williams in Baltimore. He talked me out of purchasing the smokin' Gateway computer I was about to get. The build went just fine; he told me what to buy, helped me put it together and, of course, loaded Windows 95 and a couple of other applications that I would need. Feeling confident about the process, I offered to help a friend at work build a computer. Things didn't go as smoothly.

My first critical error was that I bought parts that didn't match up (i.e., An Intel motherboard for an Advanced Micro Devices (AMD) processor and a SCSI hard drive when I needed an IDE hard drive, among other problems). When I finally got the right parts, I rushed the building process and forgot to connect some cables, tried to force my memory sticks in backward, and didn't connect the power supply to the motherboard; not surprisingly, the thing wouldn't turn on.

Obviously, I spent the next several builds on the phone with my buddy, Mike. Here's my advice to you—read the motherboard manuals and get parts that are compatible. Second, find a good tutor, like, say, US! We're the best guides you'll come across in a book.

After I placed my order, I proudly bounced the purchase off my new buddy Carlito, as it is well known around the office that he is a PC expert. From talking to him in the past, I knew that Carlito owned and operated a custom computer building company just seven years ago in Baltimore before he moved to Houston. Little did I know that my life and perspective were about to change!

Carlito took one quick look at the specifications of my new dream machine—and the $3,000 price tag—and told me to cancel the order. "I'll explain later, just cancel it while you can," he said. I immediately cancelled the order. Within the next few minutes, we discussed my exact computer needs and some of my wants. Together, we designed a system that knocked the socks off that overpriced Dell and then placed the order through a Web site that sold components. In total, I saved $1,200!

Beware the $499 PC

Dude, you get what you pay for. First of all, you always shell out more than $499 up front. Most of these deals are based on sending in mail-in rebates, a process that companies make as confusing and intimidating as doing your own taxes so you'll give up before you get any cash back. Believe it or not, many people forget to send in the paperwork or lose their receipts and never get the rebate.

The second reality behind the bargain basement PC is that if you're like most users, you can't survive with a $499 PC. You simply don't get all of the features that you need. For example, $499 PCs use integrated video and sound chips rather than higher quality video and sound cards. You also get very little memory (128 MB) and no CD burner. This computer is the bare bones—kind of like buying a car with no air conditioning or CD player—it's barely enough, but it leaves you wanting more. That's where they get you.

Three days later, the parts showed up and Carlito walked me through the same process that we've outlined for you in this book. We built the entire machine in a single afternoon and I managed to get two games of Madden NFL 2003 in before dinner (**Figure i**). By the way, you should see how this rig runs Half-Life 2; it's amazing, and the system is over a year old. Bet your Dell can't do that!

Now, here it is, a little over a year later, and I've built numerous systems for my friends and family, saving them thousands and thousands of dollars. Determined to help others conquer their computer fears and save a bundle in the process, Carlito and I teamed up to form our first company, Electric City Computers, which has now become Dude Productions, Inc. We build custom computers and have been doing quite well.

Figure i: Before Carlito helped me build my first PC, I could barely install my own operating system. After all of the parts arrived, we built this in less than a day! You can do it too. Believe me, if I can do it, anyone can do it.

The Start of a Revolution

You probably didn't know this when you bought this book, but you are a frontline recruit in a revolution designed to free people from their dependency on PC manufacturers. Once you've gone through the process we show you in this book, you'll start to see and feel the power of what we're talking about.

The evolution of home computing has brought us to the point where everyone should be building their own PCs. It's really that easy. And we're here to help you do it. We're going to open your eyes so you can see through the crap these mega corporations make billions of dollars pumping out. We're going to reveal the secrets behind why all of these companies are among the wealthiest in the world and how you can get your share of that action!

Dude, You Can Do It

Without a doubt, this is one of the most fulfilling endeavors you will ever undertake. Building a PC is educational, fun, and, most importantly, it sets you free from those big PC vendors, which means you save *money*.

You're in luck too, because there isn't a book on any shelf that can make the process easier. We're going to take you through the process of building an entire machine and installing the operating system step by step, holding your hand the whole way.

But first, we're going to explain the computer components you'll need and how they work together. Don't worry; it's not brain surgery. We'll help you determine what type of computer user you actually are, which will help you determine exactly which components you'll need to build your ideal system.

After you've determined the type of machine you want to build and created a shopping list of components, we'll give you step-by-step instructions—using plenty of pictures so you can really see what we're talking about—on how to build a better, more affordable PC than you can buy from any vendor. Along the way, we'll also throw in tips of the trade gathered from years of computer building experience (the good and bad)!

Seriously, You CAN Do It

We're not your typical computer geeks; Carlito and I are just a couple of guys who want to keep things as simple as possible, save money, and help people understand how easy building a computer really is (**Figure ii**). Most people—including us in the not-so-distant past— have no idea what parts make up a computer or what those parts actually do. That is *exactly* what big PC manufacturers depend on. Once the mystery is gone and you see the man behind the curtain, they have lost a sale. We're not going to lie to you; your very first look at the guts of a PC will be pretty intimidating (**Figure iii**). But after sticking with this book for a few chapters, you'll be talking like you invented the dang thing.

Figure ii: We're just two regular dudes, here to help. So what do you say? Ready to build your own sweet PC?

Figure iii: Fear not, friends! Although the inside of this PC may appear complex, we're going to simplify the process. By the end of Chapter 2, you'll be intimately familiar with all of the components that make your PC compute.

We hope you're excited! Do not doubt yourself in any way—you can do this! Just by picking up this book, you've proved yourself to be the kind of person who is willing to take action, which is the first and most crucial step to building your own kick-butt PC.

Now, let's take you through the other two million steps. (Just kidding, it's not *that* many.) Putting together your sweet PC is not difficult. You may struggle a little the first time, but once you learn the skill, it's like riding a bike or flying a helicopter; we're willing to bet you'll love the process!

Chapter 1

Why Build
Your Own PC?

///

Have you read the introduction to this book? If not, please stop what
you're doing right now and go back to the introduction. Stop reading.
We mean it! Once again, stop reading this chapter, go back to the
introduction, and give it a quick read. Don't worry, it's short and full
of great information.

If you're still reading—and you've actually read the introduction—then congratulations are in order. You passed the first test! You followed directions without skipping parts that may be important, which is key to building computers. We want to make this clear here in Chapter 1, right from the start, before you learn anything else. Following directions carefully is all that you need to do to successfully and skillfully build your own computer. Following procedures step by step and understanding each step prior to moving on to the next is also the best way to head off problems.

Because you've obviously already read the introduction, you should know how strongly we feel about teaching individuals *just like you* how to build your own computers. Throughout the process, there may be times when you feel that building a computer is too hard, or that you can't do it. Trust us, with our help, you *can* successfully build a computer from scratch. If that doesn't motivate you, take a look at the following top ten list we put together; these are the top ten reasons you should build your own PC rather than waste your money on a retail system.

10. You will accomplish that which the Big PC Manufacturers make billions of dollars doing.

Look, Michael Dell didn't invent the freakin' computer; he just put components together and sold them for a profit. HP has been doing it for years. Why not scrape a little off the Big PC Manufacturers' bottom line and add it to yours? If you think anyone is cutting you a break or that you're getting some sort of deal buying a computer retail, think again. Dell's profits were up 25 percent in 2004, putting it on track to become a $60 billion company in 2006—a full year ahead of schedule. Yeah, those Big PC Manufacturers really have a heart and give you your money's worth…NOT!

9. That smokin' sweet PC you're going to build will save you at least 25 percent off retail!

Sensing a theme here? When we started building our own computers, our main motivation was saving money. Then it turned into, "let's make money," which quickly turned into, "let's make money teaching people to save money."

Let's say you decide to take on this project. Will you really save $1,000 over a Big Name PC? You'll definitely save money—how much depends on the type of system you build. The more high-end you build, the more you'll save. The bonus is that you'll not only save money, but you'll build a better machine with nonintegrated parts that are easier to upgrade.

When a Big PC Manufacturer buys the same components for its systems that *you can buy very close to wholesale,* the first thing it does is mark up the components to cover its corporate overhead. Next, it charges you for labor, tacks on a few bucks for the brand name, and rolls in the shipping charges.

Why do you think retail high-end PCs are so expensive? Because Big PC Manufacturers can't build high-end systems as cheaply as you can. In this book, you'll learn how to create a machine using many of the same components that big manufacturers use in their mid- to upper-grade machines. You'll also save money because you won't have the costs associated with markup, labor, branding, and taxes (depending on where you live and what the current law is).

In the end, you'll have a much better machine for your money. That's just the truth.

8. You'll be able to upgrade your computer part-by-part instead of trashing it for a brand new one, which means, guess what? You'll save money.

You're probably thinking, "These guys sure do mention money a lot." Well, come on, isn't it important to keep that green in your pocket? Part of what you'll learn by building your own computer is that you can replace specific parts instead of buying a whole new machine when you need to upgrade. In the next year or two when your machine starts feeling its age, just swap out your motherboard and processor for the latest technology. You can still use that awesome case, monitor, keyboard, and mouse, which all tend to evolve more slowly than processors, motherboards, and video cards.

If you need an operating system upgrade and your system can still keep up, simply save all your data to a CD, DVD, or an external hard drive and load the new OS—it really is that simple.

 **Sweeet!**

Processors, video cards, and memory make great gifts for your computer-building friends. It's like buying them a new computer at a fraction of the cost!

What's the Big Deal?

GATEWAY	DUDE COMPUTER

GATEWAY	DUDE COMPUTER
☐ Proprietary case	☐ Antec Sonata Piano Black case
☐ Proprietary power supply	☐ Antec 380 Watt True Power
☐ Pentium 4 3.4 GHz	☐ AMD Athlon 64 3200+
☐ Proprietary motherboard	☐ Asus K8N motherboard
☐ 1GB PC 3200 DDR	☐ OCZ Premiere 1 GB PC3200 DDR
☐ 200 GB SATA hard drive	☐ Maxtor 200 GB SATA Hard drive
☐ 16X DVD-ROM	☐ Lite-On 16X DVD-ROM
☐ 16X dual layer DVD burner	☐ Optorite 16X dual layer DVD burner
☐ Integrated video	☐ PowerColor Radeon 9250
☐ Integrated sound	☐ Sound Blaster Audigy ES
☐ Integrated digital card reader	☐ Koutech digital card reader
Price: $980	Price: $975

If some of the above specifications don't make sense to you, don't worry, you'll learn more about SATA, DVD, CDs, GHz, and so on, in Chapter 2. If you just can't wait, then head on over there and see what they mean for yourself.

continued…

What's the Big Deal? (continued)

You may be saying to yourself, "Big deal, so I saved $5." What's not imme-
diately obvious from the above comparison is that you did much more
than that.

The Dude Computer in this comparison uses only aftermarket parts,
whereas the Big PC Manufacturers use the cheapest parts they can find
to keep costs down. With the Dude Computer, you're getting a much
higher quality machine for your money. For this system, we've chosen
a real nice case, a beefy power supply (not many power supplies in off-
the-shelf computers put out like this Antec True Power), a 64-bit processor, a top-of-the-line motherboard, high-end memory, a reputable hard
drive, and optical drives. To top it off, we resisted the temptation to use
low-quality integrated onboard video and audio, even though it would
have shaved $100 off the cost.

The Gateway in this comparison includes the things you're taught to look
for: a fast processor (Pentium 4 3.4 GHz), lots of memory (1 GB), a large
hard drive (200 GB), and a DVD burner. Well, let us be the first to tell you
that it takes much more than *that* to make a computer powerful. The
key to performance is the addition of a video card (even if it's low-end)
and a sound card because the integrated/onboard stuff takes up system
memory and processing power, drastically slowing down your computer.

We'd also like to point out that we could've gone with cheaper parts,
too. We also could've gone with less reputable vendors and cut costs by
another $100. You can do that too, although we don't recommend it.
Trust us, we've wasted many weekends trying to get cheap stuff to work.
It can be done, but you need to determine how valuable your time is to
you. The manufacturers and parts we recommend are more expensive
than most, but they work. You slap the parts in the case, turn it on, load
Windows, and wham…the thing just works.

Oh yeah, here's one cool thing we almost forgot to mention. This is kind
of a well-known secret that no one really wants to talk about. With the
Gateway, you have to pay taxes, which could cost you another $85 or so
that we didn't list here. We recommend that you buy your parts from
online stores, where you don't have to pay tax (just yet) and shipping
is fairly cheap if you get it all from the same seller. Shipping was calcu-
lated in the cost of the Dude Computer.

Now, how's that for a big deal?

7. By staying ahead of the technology, you can spread out the costs of maintaining a top-of-the line PC.

Another benefit of knowing how to upgrade your own machine is that you can anticipate and take control of the changing PC landscape before your system becomes so antiquated that you need to buy an entirely new one. One year, you spend a couple hundred bucks to update your processor and motherboard; the next year, you invest in a great 18-inch flat-panel display. You spend a little money here and there, but your computer is always up to date with the current technologies and you keep learning while you upgrade and build.

6. You can actually make money and friends at the same time.

Say your video card is still really nice, but you just want that top-of-the-line ATI ALL-IN-WONDER (AIW) RADEON soooo bad. Sell your old one to a friend who wants an upgraded video card at a discount... heck, sell it on eBay. The point here is that you can cut the price of your new card by selling your used one. Go ahead and try that with something out of one of those $499 jobs—you can't give that stuff away.

Not only can you help yourself, but you can also help your friends. Perhaps one of your friends, coworkers, or family members needs just a little extra RAM to speed along some big, processor-intensive application. Hey, you're just the person for the J.O.B. Help your friends, give them the RAM they want, and they'll come back for more. It's easy, and all the time, you're teaching people to save money and help themselves.

5. You're getting a better PC than that lazy guy down the street who thinks he got a great deal on a cool system.

Want another great reason to build your own PC? Here are two: personalization and customization. When you buy from the Big PC Manufacturers, you don't get a lot of options. If you're lucky, you may get to choose between one or two types of cases, monitors, speakers, keyboards, and mice. And colors? Beige or black. Take your pick.

When you build your own PC, the options are almost endless. If you want a case with see-through side panels, a blue back, front panel lighting, and a blue backlit keyboard, you can have it. In fact, that is exactly what Darrel built for his six-year-old son, Derek. He added a 15-inch flat panel and now the whole system fits on Derek's little desk at the end of his bunk bed and moonlights as a night-light at bedtime (**Figure 1.1**).

Figure 1.1: Derek's little gamer moonlights as a night-light.

Not only do you have creative control over how your PC looks, but you also have quality control over how it *performs.* For instance, you can focus on building a computer that's small enough to travel back and forth to college, one that plays the latest 3D games, or even one that serves as your entire entertainment system with TV-tuner and all.

4. Your mama will be so proud of you.

We wrote this to be funny, but this one can actually be a pain in the butt. We've both built computers for our parents; they love telling their friends that their son knows about computers and can build one from scratch. With this kind of publicity, you'll quickly wind-up building computers for everyone in the family who wants to save a buck. You'll also become their resident 24-hour on-call computer expert—whether you feel like one or not.

When it comes to spending hours buying parts and building systems, dude, go ahead and charge them for your time. Okay, maybe not your mom, but Aunt Betty and Uncle Fred can give you a little something for your efforts. Hey, they'll be saving a heck of a lot over a retail system *and* they've got you on the hook when it comes to tech support.

DUDE, This One Time...

One of the main reasons we decided to write this book is because so many friends have come to us with their broken computers and asked us to fix them. One such friend is Dave Scott, a fellow Coast Guard helicopter pilot. He brought us his Dell computer after months of dealing with overseas customer service phone calls to Dell's support line. He was fed up and willing to void his warranty by having *us* fix the computer.

Well, after we reinstalled Windows twice, doubled his memory, and wasted hours upon hours of time, his computer finally started working. We insist, however, that it still doesn't compare to a system he could have built himself for the same, or maybe even less, money. The computer is a little over a year old and has already been "in the shop" for at least 25 percent of its short life. What kind of Deal/Dell is that?

Was it worth it to Dave? No. But he won't build a new one because he says he doesn't have the time or the know-how to do it himself. That's what we're working to change, one person at a time.

By the time you've built your first computer, the talent and knowledge you'll have gained are sure to impress people. Trust us, we're telling you this from first-hand experience. Most folks know nothing about how their computers work or what to do when their systems go down. When they find out that you can build one from parts, well, you just became their new best buddy. These are the people who will run their computer purchases past you first or just ask you to build them new systems. Again, this is a great way to barter or simply make a little money. It's how we got started and now we own a corporation that builds computers and teaches the very process that you are about to learn.

Dude Testimonial: Maria D. Runnells

I am Maria D. Runnells, Darrel's mother. When my husband Monte and I began noticing that our computer was slow and outdated, we started thinking about buying a new one. We knew that Darrel and his partner, Carlito, had opened a business building computers for people, so I asked him what he thought about the systems we were looking at. He said, "Ma, don't buy anything until I can come over and talk to you."

I think he came over a day or two after we spoke. He first looked at our old computer and tried to see if he could fix it. Then he said, "Don't sink any money into this old thing. It would cost too much to make it work better—just let me build you one within your budget."

He asked Monte and me what we wanted out of a system. We told him that we basically play card games, pay a few bills, do some budgeting, and use the Internet a little. Darrel told us that we didn't need to spend a whole lot because we could use our monitor and all the other stuff outside the actual computer. He ordered the parts and explained that we would be getting a system that was top-of-the-line—he even showed me how much we saved over a comparable system.

The computers we were originally considering *started* at around $1,000, but seemed like more than we needed. The problem was that the cheaper ones didn't have the quality we wanted. Darrel built us a great computer for $600, and my husband says we got an excellent deal because it works better than the ones we were thinking about buying.

But the best thing about having Darrel build our new computer is that now I have his butt on the hook 24/7 if I ever have a problem. When I do, he usually says, "Look, ma, this is what you're doing wrong." Then I click whatever button he tells me to and my solitaire game starts working again.

3. You'll finally have something to talk about that people will find interesting at parties.

This may sound kooky, but if you keep your ears open, you will inevitably hear people talking about their systems and how they don't work right or how they're getting old, or maybe you'll hear that they're thinking about buying a new computer this year for Christmas or for their birthday. At this point, you can step right in and prevent someone you know from falling into the retail PC trap, because you will have the knowledge to change his or her entire perspective.

After reading this book and using our process to build a PC, you will know what you're talking about when it comes to computers and be qualified to offer advice on the subject. For example, say you're at a party loitering around the food table, snacking on nachos, when you overhear someone say, "My computer is so slow when I download and burn music CDs that it would be faster to just drive to the mall and buy the CD rather than download it from any online music store." That's when you say, "Well, what kind of Internet connection do you have? Is high-speed Internet available in your area? Is your CD burner capable of writing CDs at 52X speed? How much RAM do you have in your computer? And what kind of processor are you working with?" You say this with authority because you know that Internet connection, RAM, and processor type determine a PC's speed and that a 52X CD burner will write CDs in a couple of minutes. Do you see what we're getting at? You will have *skills*, dude.

2. You can teach others to build computers and save big bucks.

Aside from, yeah, you guessed it, saving *money,* teaching others how to build their own computers is one of the best parts of knowing how to do it yourself. It is tremendously fun to teach people this exciting and intriguing art. You'll find that young people pick this process up very quickly and understand it without any problem. In fact, it's a great project to take on with your kids.

Of course, it doesn't matter how old you are when you decide to learn how to build computers; anyone can do it. When people find out they can learn how to make something that they were going to buy anyway, pick up a very valuable talent that they can pass on to others, and save money in the process, they'll be all over you to learn how!

1. **And the # 1 reason to get excited about building your own computer:**

You can take a .000000001-percent bite out of some Big PC Manufacturer's profit margin. Doesn't that feel good?

Chapter 2

Parts Are Parts: A Look Under the Hood

///

Dude, relax, you don't need to be a computer engineer to build a PC that rivals anything from Dell, Gateway, or Compaq. All you need are the right parts, or *components,* and the know-how to piece them all together. Sure, with processor speeds constantly on the rise and a new video card hitting the market every other day, picking the right components *can* be the most time-consuming part of building your PC. But, it's also a lot of fun. Think about it: You get to customize your PC down to the very fan it uses to cool itself off. Now that's quality control!

As we warned you in the introduction, your first look under the hood might be a little intimidating. Don't sweat it too much though. This quick and dirty chapter covers all the components you need to build a killer PC, with explanations on what each component does and why you need it. Later in the book, we'll tell you exactly which parts to buy to fit the type of machine you want to build, and then we'll show you how to build it step by step.

OK, let's pop the hood and take a look.

Parts List		
No matter what type of computer you decide to build, you're going to need the same basic components. The type and quality vary, but here's a generic list for your do-it-yourself (DIY) computer. Each component is explained in greater detail in this chapter.		
☐ Case	☐ Video card	
☐ Power supply	☐ Sound card	
☐ Motherboard	☐ Storage and drives	
☐ Processor	☐ Network cards	
☐ Memory	☐ Cooling solutions	

The Processor

The processor is not just the first part you'll buy for your computer, it's the most important part. The processor functions as your computer's brain, taking all of the data flowing in and out and, well, processing it. The faster your processor, the faster your computer.

When you start shopping around for a processor, you'll find two major brands that offer an array of clock speeds. So, how do you decide which one you need? As a general rule, get as much processor as you can afford. Prices vary depending on how much speed/performance you desire. The more affordable processors start out at $100, while the newest and fastest can reach upward of $1,000.

Intel vs. AMD

The two manufacturers that currently make processors for Windows-based machines are Intel and Advanced Micro Devices (AMD). AMD processors, including the Sempron and the Athlon 64, are both great bets if you want the most performance for your money. These processors offer equal performance to the Intel Pentium 4 processors but are much more affordable.

Intel processors are more popular, but they're also pricier. If the Intel brand is important to you, or if money is no object, then you can't go wrong with an Intel Pentium 4. Don't be mistaken, however, in thinking that AMD processors are somehow inferior in performance just because they're cheaper. We use AMD processors exclusively in building our computers because we know we can get more performance from an AMD processor than from an Intel processor while saving a few bucks in the process.

Do your research and get the processor that suits your needs. Also, keep in mind that all processors need cooling, so we highly recommend that you purchase a retail version of the processor, which comes boxed with a heat sink and cooling fan designed specifically for it. If you want even more cooling for your processor, aftermarket cooling kits are available. For more information on processors, visit AMD at www.amd.com or Intel at www.intel.com.

Sweeet!

If you want to save money without sacrificing performance, buy an AMD processor. As of this writing, an Intel Pentium 4 2.8 GHz processor costs $160, whereas an AMD Athlon 64 2800+ (AMD's equivalent to the Pentium 4) only costs $125. That's a savings of $35. Plus, the AMD processor is 64-bit, while the Pentium 4 is still a 32-bit processor.

Dude Recommended: Processors

AMD Athlon 64-bit (www.amd.com): It's fast, 64-bit, and more affordable than most Intel Pentium processors. Microsoft has announced that it will upgrade Windows to 64-bit technology within the next year, which means third-party software applications are sure to follow suit. We recommend that you save yourself some money and build 64-bit technology into your computer now—before Mr. Gates makes you.

DUDE, This One Time...

When we were building a computer at band camp, we thought about using an Intel processor, but we didn't.

Debunking the Megahertz Myth

Processor speed ratings can be confusing because Intel and AMD use different numbering and naming schemes. For instance, let's take the Intel Pentium 4/3.0 GHz processor and the AMD Athlon 64 3000+. Clock speed on the Pentium 4 is 3 GHz, as the name implies. Clock speed on the Athlon 3000+ is 2 GHz. You're thinking that the Pentium 4 should be faster, right? Well, it's not.

AMD has embarked on a mission to shatter the megahertz myth. Stated simply, the megahertz myth is the belief that clock frequency (GHz) is the only true measure of real processor performance. In reality, processor performance should be measured by how quickly an application completes an assigned task, not just by clock speed.

Here's an easy way to look at it:

Processor Performance = Clock Speed × Work Accomplished per Clock Cycle

What it boils down to is that AMD has made its processors more efficient by designing them to complete more work per cycle. Thus, an Intel Pentium 4/3.0 GHz processor and an AMD Athlon 64 3000+ are directly comparable in performance. Refer to AMD's Web site at www.amd.com for further explanation of the megahertz myth.

DUDE, This One Time...

We took on a new project and decided to try to build a $499 PC. You know what's coming next, right? We sent back three motherboards, a set of memory, and two cases because we just couldn't make all those cheap parts work together. Take our word for it; do *not* try this at home.

The Motherboard

Your body has a central nervous system to keep all of its components running smoothly; a computer has a motherboard (**Figure 2.1**). When choosing your motherboard, keep in mind that every component in your computer connects to it, so compatibility is the name of the game. In other words, the motherboard must support and work with whatever you plan on plugging into it. This match game may sound difficult, but as long as you pay close attention to motherboard specifications, you won't have any problems.

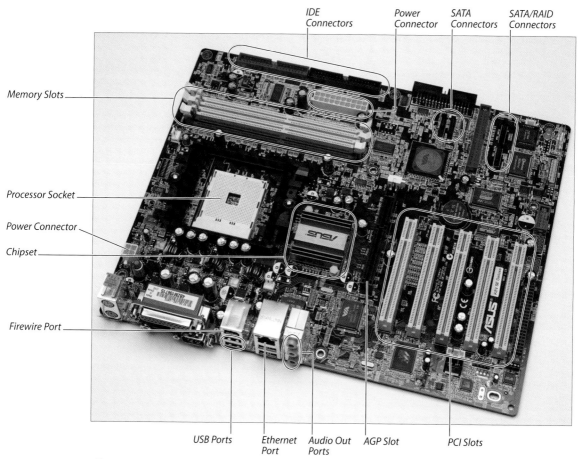

Figure 2.1: The motherboard serves as your computer's central nervous system—all of your components plug into it. Be sure to pick your motherboard and processor at the same time because motherboards are built to work with specific processors.

Motherboards are designed to work with specific processors, so make sure that you make your motherboard and processor selections at the same time. That said, the first step in any computer project is to pick the processor, because that determines how powerful your computer will be and how much you're going to spend. Your entire budget for building a PC is based on your processor choice. Do you want a Porsche or a beat-up Ford Pinto? One is going to cost you more, but it will get you where you want to go much faster.

The next step is to choose a motherboard—from a reputable manufacturer—that is compatible with the processor you've chosen. After you have your processor and motherboard picked out, you can order the remaining parts. The rest of your components are pretty standard, meaning their formats and types are common among most motherboard designs. As always though, it can't hurt to double-check compatibility. Don't worry; as soon as you forget to do this one time and buy the wrong part, double-checking compatibility will become second nature.

The following terms cover the major specifications that you'll need to consider when choosing a motherboard.

Sweeet!

Your motherboard must be compatible with your processor, or nothing works.

Sweeet!

Our favorite motherboard and processor combo is an AMD Athlon 64 with an ASUS motherboard. For more details, check out www.amd.com and www.ASUS.com. For cooler tips, visit our Web site at www.dudecomputers.com.

The Socket

The *socket* is where your processor plugs into your motherboard. The *socket type* refers to the configuration of your processor slot. If you purchase a motherboard that has a different socket type than your processor, it will either not fit or not work . . . kind of like a 15-inch tire on a 16-inch rim. If you're having trouble finding the socket on your motherboard, either consult the motherboard diagram or look for the big, beige, flat, square thing located close to the center of the motherboard. It has about a million tiny holes in it as well as a very small open/close metal lever.

There are many socket types available, many of which depend on whether you're using an Intel or an AMD processor. We don't use or pretend to know a lot about Intel processors, so let's talk about the socket types available for AMD processors.

For the AMD Athlon 64 processors, the sockets available are Socket 754, Socket 939, and Socket 940. Socket 940 is being phased out and replaced by Socket 939 because it required Error Correcting Code

Sweeet!

Other than Intel and AMD, which design custom chipsets to work with their particular processors, chipset manufacturers come up with their own designs to maximize the performance of various processors. Most of these manufacturers design chipsets for both AMD and Intel processors. Still, when buying a motherboard, make sure that its chipset works with your particular processor type. In other words, if you buy one of AMD's premium Athlon 64 processors, check your motherboard specifications to make sure it supports that processor.

(ECC) memory (which is more expensive and not required unless you're running a server). To get to the point, if you buy a processor that is Socket 754–compatible, for example, make sure your motherboard CPU socket is a Socket 754. How do you check this? You guessed it! Read the specs on the motherboard box or check the company's Web site.

Chipsets

A *chipset* controls the data that flows through your motherboard and processor, ensuring that all data gets routed to the proper components. Popular chipset makers include *n*VIDIA, ATI, Intel, VIA, SIS, and AMD. These companies are always tweaking and updating their chipsets in order to get an edge up on performance.

Visit our Web site for links to great hardware review sites such as www.tomshardware.com and www.anandtech.com. We rely on the expert reviews at these sites to decide which chipsets to use for our *own* computer builds. Currently our favorite chipsets are *n*VIDIA nForce 3 Ultra and VIA K8T800 Pro. Keep in mind, however, that there is a negligible performance difference between the *n*VIDIA and the VIA chipsets; they trade top spots all the time. We just prefer these two chipsets because they get the better reviews at many of our favorite hardware review Web sites.

Motherboards with these chipsets are also more expensive—once again, you get what you pay for. What we stress to computer builders is that you purchase a motherboard from a reputable manufacturer (as we mentioned earlier, our favorite is ASUS), and make sure that the sockets and processor match.

Memory Slots

Memory slots on your motherboard only accept the type of memory that they are designed to use. If you buy the wrong type of memory, it simply will not fit due to the pin configuration. Double-data-rate (DDR) memory is the most commonly used, with DDR2 slowly making its way into the market. Most motherboards have three to four memory slots.

Universal Serial Bus (USB) Ports

You use *USB ports* (**Figure 2.2**) to connect external (peripheral) pieces of hardware—including digital cameras, printers, personal digital assistants (PDAs), and cell phones—to your computer. Make sure you have enough USB ports to connect everything you expect to use and add a couple extra to cover the things you haven't thought of. Four USB ports may work for most people, but six is probably safer. If the need arises and you have a motherboard expansion slot (PCI slot), you can always add an expansion card that will give you two more USB ports for a total of eight.

Figure 2.2: USB ports peek out through the back of your case and allow you to connect a wide range of peripherals—ranging from your keyboard and mouse to an LCD flat panel monitor—to your computer.

Integrated Sound Chip

Many motherboards come with integrated sound chips, also called *onboard audio*, but we recommend buying a sound card anyway. Why? Onboard audio is notoriously unreliable. We've had a mere 50 percent success rate with it. Also, when—and if—you do get onboard audio to work, you're treated to crackling noises and distortion at high volumes. A sound card is the perfect solution.

Sweeet!

Get yourself a motherboard with no onboard video, purchase a Radeon 9250 video card for about $40, and get the show on the road.

DUDE, This One Time...

I (Carlito) tried to build a computer from spare parts; I wanted to spend absolutely as little money as possible because I was building this PC for my daughter, Kelsie, who was five at the time. All she and her brother, Kyle, needed the computer to do was play the latest Barbie Princess and Hot Wheels racing games. So I went ahead and decided only to upgrade the motherboard and processor and reuse the memory, CD-ROM, floppy drive, hard drive, memory, case, and power supply from an older computer.

Against my better judgment, I bought a highly integrated motherboard that had onboard sound and video and kept my upgrade costs (including the processor) under $100. I got the parts three days later and spent the next two weeks trying to get the darn thing to work. I never did. I wound up buying a new motherboard and video card and selling the computer because I was so frustrated I wanted the thing out of my house.

For as little as $15, you can add a sound card to your setup that provides much better sound than what onboard audio produces. To use a sound card instead of the integrated sound chips that come with your motherboard, you just need to turn off onboard audio in the BIOS setup.

Integrated Video Chip

Some cheaper and highly integrated motherboards come with built-in video chips that are often referred to as *onboard video*. These chips provide basic video capabilities—such as viewing spreadsheets or documents that don't have any images—that work well enough in the 2D world.

Now, as far as viewing spreadsheets and simple images goes, you won't be able to tell the difference between onboard video and a video card. The more (much more) noticeable difference comes into play when you're surfing a graphic-intensive Web site, working in Photoshop, or playing 3D games. We've also noticed that LCD flat panel monitors don't like onboard video; in fact, they don't display the crisp images and bright colors we see when we use video cards.

Manufacturers use these low-end video chips because high-end digital video processors are expensive, large, and drive the price of the motherboard through the roof.

If your machine has *only* the onboard video that comes with the motherboard, surfing the Internet and viewing or editing digital photos will be painful and slow. Don't even try to play a game of Far Cry; Windows will slur as if it just downed four martinis in one sitting; it may even freeze up on you. Basically, onboard video is terrible and we do not recommend using it. Even $40 video cards perform exponentially better than onboard video.

Accelerated Graphics Port (AGP)

The majority of the video cards available today plug in to your motherboard through the accelerated graphics port (AGP). AGP-based video cards have replaced PCI (Peripheral Component Interconnect) slot-based video cards because of their greater bandwidth capacity to and from the main memory; basically, they're faster!

PCI Slots

PCI slots allow you to connect sound cards, network cards, controller cards, and even USB add-on cards to your computer. Most motherboards provide you with plenty, but you need to make sure you have at least four—one for sound and three extra to accommodate future expansion.

PCI Xpress Slot

PCI Xpress is a newer, better, faster type of PCI slot. Because it's so much faster, PCI Xpress is certain to replace both PCI and AGP technologies somewhere down the line. The technology is still new, however, and needs time to mature, so don't expect PCI and AGP slots and components to go away any time soon.

LAN Controller

A LAN (large area network) controller is a chip on the motherboard that is used to connect your computer to various types of broadband Internet connections and to other computers or networks. Make sure not to confuse the LAN controller with your Ethernet connection. The LAN controller is a chip on your motherboard, while the Ethernet connection is the port on the back of your computer that allows you to connect your computer via a LAN cable to the Internet, another computer, or a network.

Typically, onboard LAN controllers are dependable and can save you money. Most motherboards come with an integrated LAN controller, but if you're upgrading an older computer and trying to set up cable modem service, be sure to check your motherboard specifications to ensure you have one. If you don't, you'll need to purchase a network card.

 **Sweeet!**

Although PCI Xpress seems to be the wave of the future for video cards and many other add-on cards, it is not yet a mature technology and doesn't provide a significant performance increase to warrant using it at this time. Don't be a guinea pig. Check our Web site at www.dudecomputers.com for updates and recommendations on this technology.

Sweeet!

You can still purchase IDE hard drives, but because of the slight cost difference, we recommend you step up to the latest and greatest. SATA is a new data transfer technology for hard drives, but we love it and recommend it even though it's still fairly new. Data transfer isn't significantly faster yet, but it makes assembling your PC much neater and easier. You'll have less cable clutter because SATA cables are much thinner and more rigid. Plus, it just looks cool. You want your sweet PC to look cool, right? Your motherboard specifications will tell you if your board will accommodate SATA hard drives.

DUDE, This One Time...

We ordered parts for a new computer build and forgot to check the specs—yes, we're human too. When the parts arrived and we began to assemble them, we realized we couldn't hook up the hard drive because the motherboard only supported the old IDE connectors. Learn from *our* mistakes and don't forget to check the specs! Also, keep in mind that if you get a SATA hard drive, you'll need a motherboard to connect it to. In other words, don't forget to get a motherboard with a SATA controller.

Form Factor

A motherboard's *form factor* is basically the size and shape of the board. The two main motherboard form factors are ATX and MicroATX. The key here is to make sure your motherboard fits inside your case. An ATX motherboard fits in a mid-tower and bigger. A MicroATX motherboard fits in a mini-tower as well as all larger towers. If you're using a mini-tower, chances are only a MicroATX motherboard will fit. The main advantage to going with an ATX form factor instead of the micro model is that you get several more expansion slots.

RAID

RAID stands for Redundant Array of Independent (or Inexpensive) Disks. RAID setups use two or more hard drives to either increase system performance or provide fault tolerance in case your system crashes or fails. RAID drives are commonly used in servers but are not necessary in personal computers. RAID has become popular in the high-end, do-it-yourself market, but in our opinion, using RAID in such cases is overkill and better left to the PC enthusiast.

SATA/IDE Controller

SATA (Serial ATA) and IDE (Integrated Drive Electronics) controllers are the primary interfaces used to connect hard drives, floppy drives, and optical drives to your computer. IDE has long been the standard. SATA is a newcomer and—just as the name implies—is a serial connection for your hard drive. SATA provides faster data transfer and an easier connection interface than IDE. Your CD, DVD, and floppy drives hook up to your motherboard through IDE controllers, but your hard drive will likely connect through the SATA controller.

The Case

Like people, computer cases come in all shapes, sizes, and colors, and they are also made of different materials. All cases, however, share one common trait—they all support ATX motherboards. ATX is nothing fancy; as we said before, it just refers to motherboard dimensions. The only thing you need to know is whether or not your motherboard will fit in your case. MicroATX motherboards fit in a mini-tower or bigger, whereas an ATX motherboard fits in a mid- or full-tower.

Cases come in the following four sizes: full-tower, mid-tower, mini-tower, and SFF (Small Form Factor).

The Full-Tower

The full-tower is the biggest case you can buy. The main advantage to using the Incredible Hulk of computer cases is the amount of room available inside. Buy a full-tower if you need space for lots of components or if you require large amounts of airflow for cooling high-powered processors and video cards. Full-towers are also the easiest

to work with because you have more room to move around in when you're installing components (a blessing for people with big hands or those who aren't exactly deft at manipulating small tools).

The one major drawback to using a full-tower case is its large footprint—this means it takes up a lot of space and can't be discreetly hidden. You can also forget about throwing it in your backpack and taking it to class with you. But if you aren't all that concerned about making more room in your life—and under your desk—for a bigger box, then the full-tower could well be a good choice for your first build.

The Mid-Tower

The mid-tower is a great compromise between the mini-tower and the full-tower (**Figure 2.3**). It offers the best of both worlds because it doesn't take up as much space as the full tower, but is still large enough to allow for many components and sufficient airflow to cool off high-powered parts. Although you won't have as much room to work in, the mid-tower is an excellent choice for most builds.

Figure 2.3: The mid-tower is the perfect choice for anyone who doesn't want his computer to be too big or too small, but rather, just right. It's the best of both worlds. We prefer the mid-tower and SFF over the other case sizes. For the mid-tower, our favorite case is the Antec Sonata.

The Mini-Tower

The mini-tower, which is about half the size of a full-tower, is the second smallest case you can buy. This case size leaves a fairly small footprint, but it still offers ample room for multiple drives and internal components. Be aware, however, that as interior space decreases, flexibility decreases along with it. In addition, heat, which slows down your components and can make your entire PC sluggish, starts to become more of a problem. It is also much more difficult to work inside the mini-tower because of the smaller case size, so keep that in mind if you have trouble pulling off precision work.

Sweeet!

If you're using a high-end processor and/or video card, plan on installing multiple fans inside your mini-tower to help cool your components.

The SFF

The SFF is the latest case trend in the do-it-yourself computer market (**Figure 2.4**). Many times referred to as *space-savers*, these cases have a very small footprint and are usually shaped like a cube or small rectangle.

Figure 2.4: Can't afford a laptop? An SFF case is almost as portable and even more powerful. This is a great option for college students who come home for the weekends. SFFs outperform laptops and are easily shuttled back and forth from home to your dorm room.

Can't afford a laptop? An SFF is small and light enough to serve as a powerful alternative. Some SFFs even come with custom handles, carrying cases, or book bags. Students love these things because they can use them for their studies all day, and then take them to gaming parties or even home for the weekend. The biggest advantage to having an SFF over a laptop is that an SFF can host a lot more computer power for a lot less money.

Many SFF cases come with preconfigured, highly integrated motherboards. They also offer creative cooling solutions that are much different than the standard heat sink and fan. Onboard video and audio are integrated onto the motherboard to facilitate cooling and to keep size down, and most SFF designs also limit you to one CD or DVD drive. It's the price you pay to keep your machine compact.

SFF case designs are changing very rapidly; because this market is growing in popularity, manufacturers are supplying options to meet all needs and price ranges.

 Dude Recommended:
Case Manufacturers

Antec (www.antec.com): Antec cases are well designed, with the builder in mind. They have smooth edges, great materials, logically placed racks, slide-in rails for your drives, great power supplies (some of the best in the industry), and the price for these cases is fair considering the quality and care that goes into them. In other words, the Antec case is hard to beat unless you're willing to spend a lot more money for a small jump in quality.

Shuttle (www.shuttle.com): These cases look amazing and are very easy to build. Shuttle was the innovator in the SFF field and the first to introduce these types of cases. Shuttle's SFFs are definitely more refined with stable power supplies, innovative cooling solutions, and well-designed motherboards. Plus, their case design is the easiest to tear apart and reassemble that we've ever come across.

Lian Li (www.lian-li.com): These cases use the highest quality materials (high grade aluminum); they have motherboard trays that slide in and out for easy installation; they come with built-in ball bearing cooling fans; and they've got a spacious interior. Their only downfall is that they're also very expensive. But if you want the Lexus of computer cases, this is it.

Material Differences

As we mentioned earlier, cases are made from all kinds of materials. Your cheaper cases are made of thin steel; the more expensive cases come in aluminum. For low- to mid-range applications, a steel case will work just fine. For mid- to high-end machines and your gamers, the aluminum helps tremendously with cooling. We can't stress this point enough: If you're building a high-end system, spend the extra money to get a high quality case. Companies such as Antec, Lian Li, and Thermaltake, just to name a few of our favorites, produce quality cases.

When deciding on a case, you'll also want one that has smooth edges, room for airflow, solid power supplies, good aesthetics, a number of drive bays for CD and DVD drives, and front USB and audio ports if you can get 'em.

Sweeet!

If you want the best, buy an aluminum case. The best cases are made of aluminum for two reasons: They dissipate heat better, which makes the parts last longer and work better, and they look way cooler than your typical steel boxes.

The Power Supply

The power supply is often a computer's most overlooked, yet most vital, component (**Figure 2.5**). Power supplies are measured in watts, but watts aren't everything. You want a well-built power supply that uses quality fans to keep it cool because nothing, and we mean *nothing*, causes your computer to fail faster than a cheap power supply.

Figure 2.5: Power supplies are the most overlooked component in a PC. A cheap power supply will ruin your day—it could make your operating system install stall out, damage your video card, slow down your motherboard, and so on. Don't skimp on your power supply. Repeat. Don't skimp on your power supply.

In our years of experience building computers, faulty power supplies have been at the root of many of the problems we've encountered. During one particular build, a faulty power supply was at the root of why Windows wouldn't install properly. The computer would restart itself because the power supply was heating up and it needed to cool itself. Trust us, you don't want to spend $1,000 on a computer and have it damaged or not work correctly because you skimped on the power supply.

If you lay out the cash for a premium case, you'll probably have to buy the power supply separately—get a good one. We'll tell you when you can cut costs and it's not here. There are many good companies that sell power supplies including Antec, Fortron Source, Enermax, Sparkle, Thermaltake, and Vantec—just stay away from their low-end power supplies. Get a power supply that's at least 350 watts and is of medium- to high-end quality. Anything smaller, or of lesser quality, may not provide stable, continuous power to your system.

Medium quality power supplies start out at $50, with the high-end ones reaching up to $150. A quality power supply will have duel cooling fans (ball bearing is better) and provide stable power with minimum noise—you don't want the thing to sound like a helicopter hovering overhead. Fan speed control is also a nice feature—it keeps noise down and speeds up the fans only when the power supply gets hot.

Memory

Memory is the place where your processor conducts all of its work, serving as a temporary storage place for data and information that's being processed (**Figure 2.6**). Memory plays a critical role in your computer's performance, so make sure you have enough and that it's of high quality. We recommend that you stick with the major vendors, such as OCZ Technology, Kingston Technology Company, and Crucial (a division of Micron), and avoid the generic house brand memory that is available across the Internet.

Figure 2.6: This is 1 GB of OCZ High Performance PC3200 RAM. This is higher-end memory and we only recommend it if you are building an SFF PC or a gaming PC where you'll be tasking your memory and cooling is a top priority.

The biggest problems we've seen with house brand memory is that PCs become sluggish when running processor- and memory-intensive applications, such as Photoshop and some games. The generic memory works just fine for typing up Excel spreadsheets or a grocery list, but when you really need it to perform, it won't. We've also seen generic memory not even work with different motherboards; ASUS motherboards are notorious for not accepting generic memory.

You'll have to match up your memory to your motherboard, so read your motherboard specifications and make sure you buy the right stuff. Most motherboards accept 184-pin DDR memory with newer boards introducing DDR2, the next generation DDR memory. We recommend a minimum of 512 MB of DDR RAM with 1,024 MB or 1 GB being optimal if you can afford it.

A decent amount of memory (512 MB) will run you about $80, and 1 GB will cost about $140. If you get the higher-end memory (recommended only for you gamers and graphics guys), you'll probably pay close to twice the price of the regular good stuff.

 **Sweeet!**

DDR2 is new and not mature. Save your hard-earned cash and stick with DDR memory until the market dictates that it's time to upgrade.

 Sweeet!

Get the good stuff—cheap-o memory will not do. In fact, if you want your rig to look even better, get the stuff with heat spreaders. Heat spreaders are soft metal strips that attach to the memory chips. They dissipate heat by spreading it over a larger area and transferring it from the actual chip into the ambient air in the box. Heat spreaders also make the guts of your PC look cooler. Memory chips are basically boring little green cards with black chips on them. The heat spreaders can be blue, platinum, gold, and other fancy colors.

Dude Recommended: Memory

OCZ (www.ocztechnology.com): We've used this memory extensively in our more expensive computer builds. OCZ provides a little better pricing than its high-end competitors, plus we like how it looks and we've yet to receive a stick of memory from them that was defective.

Kingston (www.kingston.com): Kingston and Crucial—the big boys of the memory business—produce stable, quality memory, including a high-end line with heat spreaders and more aggressive timings. Their products, however, are more expensive than OCZ's comparable high-end memory.

Crucial (www.crucial.com): See the explanation above.

Corsair (www.corsairmemory.com): From the bottom to the top of its product line, Corsair's pricing and quality are consistent with the market.

GeIL (www.geilusa.com): We've had limited experience with GeIL but have many friends and peers who swear by its products.

Video Cards

The *video card* is responsible for all the images you see on your computer monitor (**Figure 2.7**). The better the video card (and usually, the more expensive too!), the better and faster your images appear onscreen. The most expensive video card on the market right now will set you back about $600, while the cheapest—still better than onboard graphics chips—comes in at around $40. A good video card is key for hard-core gamers because of the immense processing power needed to display the complex 3D images in today's games.

Figure 2.7: This is a PowerColor Radeon 9800 Pro video card, which includes more memory and a better cooling solution than many other video cards. Some of it is pure aesthetics, but the cooling solution is the key to keeping the high-end GPU trucking along.

ATI (www.ati.com) and *n*VIDIA (www.nvidia.com) supply the two major graphics chips for video cards. Both produce outstanding graphics processing units (GPU), so you can't go wrong with either. Graphics technologies are always changing, however, so make sure you do some research before deciding on a video card. You'll find that plenty of other companies make GPUs, but they haven't been around long and are unproven. Hold off on these new GPU makers until they've proven themselves in the marketplace. Right now, stick with ATI or *n*VIDIA.

Choosing the Right Video Card

As you'll see when you begin surfing the Web for a video card, you won't be hurting for lack of choice. So how do you know which one to buy? Ask yourself these two questions:

1. Will my computer be a gaming machine?

2. How much am I willing to spend?

Sweeet!

We've used both ATI and *n*VIDIA video cards in the past, but recently we've leaned toward favoring ATI cards. There is nothing wrong with *n*VIDIA cards; we just prefer the software that comes with the ATI cards. PowerColor makes great ATI cards with easy-to-use software at affordable prices.

Sweeet!

Our hands-down favorite video card is the Radeon 9800 Pro. We can't say enough nice things about this video card. We use it a lot since it recently dropped in price by over $100. A year ago, maybe less, it was ATI's most expensive card. Today, it costs just a little over $200. If you've got some extra cash, add the "All in Wonder" features, which include a TV tuner.

If you plan on using your computer for basic office work, email, and Internet purposes, save yourself a little money and get a card that costs no more than $50 to $70. The lower-end ATI Radeon and *n*VIDIA FX cards give you adequate video processing power, without breaking your bank. These cards qualify as budget gaming cards, so you'll even be able to play most games—just don't expect the fast frame rates and high resolution you would get from a premium video card.

At no point should you go with video chips that are integrated on many cheaper motherboards. Onboard video is very cheap, but it slows your computer down big time because it takes computer processing power and memory away from your computer. Trust us, if you go with onboard video, you'll regret it.

If you'll be using your computer to play games, expect to pay $350 or more for a high quality video card. This may seem like a lot of money, but it's the price you pay if you want to play. If you want to game but don't have the big bucks, you can compromise with a decent $100 to $200 video card, which lets you play most games at reasonable frame rates and resolution—just don't expect to win any online tournaments.

Dude Recommended:
Video Card Manufacturers

PowerColor (www.power-color.com): PowerColor tweaks its cards to eek out a little extra performance and also produces video cards with ATI GPUs that are more affordable than the ones you get directly from ATI. Plus, the software package that comes with the cards includes free and/or demo versions of the latest 3D games.

ATI (www.ati.com): ATI makes a GPU in addition to producing its own cards. The software package that comes with the cards is unbeatable. Get an ATI card and see for yourself.

Sapphire (www.sapphiretech.com): Sapphire cards are comparable to PowerColor cards, although they're a touch pricier. Sapphire has more product lines than PowerColor, so you also get more to choose from.

Sound Cards

Sound cards (**Figure 2.8**) process audio data and send it off to your speakers. As we said earlier, onboard audio chips are bad—don't use them. Onboard audio and video tie up processor resources, so even if you get yourself a cheap $15 sound card to support your two-channel speakers, you'll be better off. Onboard sound chips are also unreliable and tend to fail when you least expect it. Plus, they sound terrible with their annoying crackling and hissing. Get yourself a decent sound card—your computer and your ears will thank you for it.

Figure 2.8: Creative Sound Blaster sound cards cost more than most, but are worth every penny. Your ears will thank you for the crystal clear audio.

Creative Labs is a well known, proven sound card manufacturer that currently owns most of the sound card market. Creative Sound Blaster sound cards are a bit pricier than most, but you get much better sound from them. Before buying a sound card, however, check that it will support your speakers. Many sound cards provide 4-channel or even 6-channel support ranging from 2.1 to 7.1 speaker systems. If you don't already have speakers, don't forget to get some to go with your new sound card. Check out www.creative.com for some cool gear.

Storage and Drives

If you're creating a bare-bones computer system, you'll need a minimum of a hard drive and a CD-ROM drive. Many people, however, also like to stock their machines with floppy drives, DVD drives, and CD/DVD burners. We'll recommend some configurations using these drives and burners in later chapters.

Floppy Drives

Yes, floppy drives are going the route of the dinosaur, but they're not extinct yet, and therefore, we recommend that you install one (**Figure 2.9**). Floppy drives used to be the only way to get files from one computer to another. These days, they're used mainly for software installation or as a backup to external drives and CD-ROMs. Although many computers no longer come with floppy drives, we recommend you install one since the cost is minimal and doing so allows easy access to small documents.

Figure 2.9: Floppy drives are pretty cheap to install and can come in handy for lugging around small files. Some of the big name PC vendors are phasing these out, but for $15, we think they're still worth keeping around.

Hard Drives

The *hard drive* is a permanent place where you store everything on your computer, from your operating system to your digital music collection (**Figure 2.10**). When we say permanent, we mean that your hard drive will keep all of the data stored there until you deliberately choose to erase it. Because all of your crucial information is stored on the hard drive, the consequences are very serious if it fails. For this reason, we use and recommend an external USB hard drive to store critical data such as photos, school work, office work, music, financial info, and so on.

Figure 2.10: Get the biggest hard drive you can buy. You can never have enough storage. Stick with reputable manufacturers; we recommend Maxtor.

Sweeet!

Does size matter? Not always, but get as much as you can afford to buy when shopping for a hard drive. You can never have enough storage space and you'll regret it later when you have to add a second drive or install a new internal drive.

You will not be storing your operating system or other applications on your external hard drive, just important data that you don't want to lose. Make sure you get enough storage space; we recommend a minimum of 80 GB (gigabytes) for your internal hard drive. Your external hard drive can be as big as you need it to be. Remember, for your external hard drive, it's better that you be conservative and get a bigger hard drive than you need.

Dude Recommended:
Hard Drive Manufacturers

Maxtor (www.maxtor.com): We really like Maxtor's Ultra series; you get plenty of bang for the buck and the customer service is outstanding.

Western Digital (www.westerndigital.com): Maker of the only 10,000 rpm (revolutions per minute) drive we came across. While most SATA hard drives run/spin at 7,200 rpm, Western Digital has released an SATA hard drive (code name "Raptor") that runs at 10,000 rpm. We've built a couple of machines with these drives and they are indeed a little faster. It's not that noticeable to the average computer user though. The price you pay for this slight bump in speed isn't really worth it unless you're building the most expensive gaming computer money can buy and are really trying to squeeze every ounce of performance out of it.

Seagate (www.seagate.com): If you want a company that's been around forever and makes reliable drives, this is it.

Optical Drives

These drives are read-only, meaning you can't use them to save any information to a compact disc (CD) or digital video disc (DVD). *Optical drives* simply allow you to open files already stored on CDs and DVDs on your computer. So, why bother getting a drive with such limited usefulness? You need one to install your operating system. We've had great success with Lite-On IT DVD drives, which we've found to be both affordable and reliable.

Dude Recommended:
Optical Drive Manufacturers

Optorite (www.optorite.com): We love Optorite's high quality, afford-able drives. We give Optorite the edge over Lite-On IT because aestheti-cally, we think its drives look cooler!

Lite-On IT (www.liteonit.com): Lite-On IT makes great drives that are on par with Optorite drives when it comes to quality and price.

Plextor (www.plextor.com): Plextor has been in the market for a long time; in fact, we used Plextor drives for the first computers we ever built. Plextor drives have a sturdier tray mechanism, but you pay for the qual-ity. In order to keep costs down, we recommend the above drives over Plextor drives because—although Plextor drives seem to be built bet-ter—we've never had an Optorite or Lite-On IT drive fail on us.

 **Sweeet!**

We like having two drives, one DVD and one CD or DVD burner. It provides a lot of flexibility.

 Sweeet!

If you plan on doing a lot of video edit-ing with your machine, go for the DVD burner. Movies take up a lot of space and might not fit entirely onto a CD when you're done. Plus, you want to be able to watch your Academy Award winner on your own TV, don't you?

CD/DVD Burners

In addition to allowing you access to files on CD and DVD discs, *CD* and *DVD burners* allow you to—as the name implies—burn (*write*) data to CDs and DVDs (**Figure 2.11**). CDs hold 650 to 700 MB of data while DVDs can pack in between 4.7 and 9.4 GB. That's a big difference, so make sure you think about that carefully when deciding what type of burner to install in your new computer. DVDs can store much more information, but the drives and storage are more expensive.

Figure 2.11: A typical CD can hold 650 to 700 MB of data, but a DVD can hold even more— 4.7 to 9.4 GB. Think about it before you decide which type of burner to install.

Sweeet!

We've got one word for you: integrated. Why spend $30 for an Ethernet card when many of the nicer motherboards come with built-in, integrated Ethernet controllers? Save your hard-earned cash and get a faster AMD processor.

Sweeet!

If you plan on networking through this computer, get a motherboard with two Ethernet connections. Why? You can't be on the Internet and networked to another PC at the same time with only one Ethernet connection.

Network Cards

Modem cards and Ethernet cards are both types of *network cards.* Modem cards let you dial into your Internet Service Provider (ISP) through your phone line. Ethernet cards enable you to hook up to a high-speed Internet connection or connect to a LAN.

We really don't recommend going the dial-up route, unless you're the type of person who finds waiting in bumper-to-bumper traffic relaxing. Dial-up is sloooow. Really, really, really slow. Still, if you insist, or if you don't have access to a high-speed Internet connection, you'll need to get a modem card (**Figure 2.12**). Plenty of vendors sell modem cards and it really doesn't matter which one you get. Basically, you just want one that works, and most do.

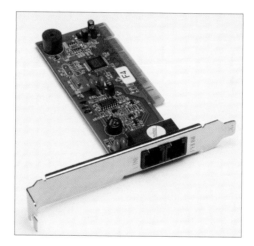

Figure 2.12: If you like to take things slow, dial up to the Internet through your phone line. You'll need a modem card like this one to do it though.

If you plan on spending any time at all online, we recommend that you connect through either DSL or a cable modem. We prefer the cable modem because it's faster and not much more expensive. With either choice, you'll need an Ethernet card to connect your computer to the high-speed connection—unless your motherboard has that function integrated. Most motherboards come with an onboard LAN chip, so you may not need to purchase an add-on Ethernet card. Contact your local cable company for more details—many times they'll give you an Ethernet card and/or cable modem for free!

Cooling Solutions

When we talk about cooling solutions, we're referring to—you guessed it—fans. If you decide to purchase an OEM (Original Equipment Manufacturer) processor, or if you want to protect that expensive processor with a better cooling solution, then you need an aftermarket heat sink and fan. Don't panic. We're not asking you to do anything illegal—*aftermarket* is completely different from *black market*. Feel better?

Aftermarket Processor Coolers

For most of you, the cooler that comes boxed with your processor will work just fine and provide all the fresh air your hard-working components need to stay cool. There's no need for you to waste money on an aftermarket cooler.

On the other hand, if you're a hard core gamer or even a PC enthusiast with a penchant for adding a bunch of extra cards to your system, your components may need a little extra help chilling out. In either of these cases, an aftermarket cooler would be just the ticket (**Figure 2.13**).

Figure 2.13: The Polo 735 is one of our favorite aftermarket coolers. Hard-core gamers and PC enthusiasts are the only ones who really need aftermarket coolers, such as this one. Most folks are fine with the stock coolers that come packaged with processors. Be aware, however, that stock coolers only come with retail boxed processors; OEM processors do not have stock coolers.

Sweeet!

All retail boxed processors come with a stock cooler. These coolers are good enough for everyday use, but if you plan on doing any graphic or processor intensive work, you'll need an aftermarket cooler to get rid of extra heat. Most normal users don't need an aftermarket cooler, although they look much "cooler" than the stock ones.

If this book is your first step toward becoming a PC enthusiast, then chances are an extreme cooling solution lies somewhere in your future. When shopping for an aftermarket processor cooler, look for quiet, ball bearing fans and high quality heat sinks. Generally, the more money you spend, the better the cooler. You'll be fine if you can stay within a $20 to $35 price range. Anything more is a waste of money and anything less may not be good enough.

Case Fans

Case fans, which provide cooling to all of your components, are also great to have (**Figure 2.14**). Everything in your computer generates heat, so case fans act as insurance that all of your components stay nice and cool. As with aftermarket coolers, look for case fans that are quiet and of high quality. Also, check to make sure that the fan you buy fits on the mounting area inside your case.

Figure 2.14: Case fans double as cheap insurance against overheating by helping to move air inside your case. They help keep vital components, such as memory, video cards, and processors, cooler.

Unless you're really trying to save money, you should incorporate at least an intake cooling fan and place it at the front of the case on the inside. The cases we recommend come with at least one cooling fan. Case fans costs about $7 and are really worth having. We also highly recommend an exhaust fan, which you would place at the back of the case. Both the intake and exhaust fan are ideal because together, they create a cooling flow of air. You're pulling cold air into the case with the intake fan and you're blowing out the warm air via the exhaust fan. This is, however, somewhat noisy, so most of the time we use just one or the other to keep the noise down.

Dude Recommended:
Cooler Manufacturers

Thermaltake (www.thermaltake.com): Thermaltake has always made high quality aftermarket coolers for processors. With the release of the Polo 735, we think they offer the more innovative products too.

Cooler Master (www.coolermaster.com): As the name implies, Cooler Master makes high quality standard coolers, although its products aren't as innovative as we'd like.

Vantec (www.vantecusa.com): We don't have much experience with these coolers, but we have computer-building friends who have had great success with them and who really like them. We can't know it all!

 Sweeet!

Don't forget the thermal compound. The surface of your processor and heat sink are never entirely flat. Thermal compound is a paste that does two things: First, it fills in the tiny gaps or imperfections in the surface of your processor and heat sinks. Second, its properties allow for better heat transfer between your heat sink and processor.

Why do you need it? Because you want to transfer as much heat as possible from your processor to the heat sink and then into the air through the fan on the heat sink. Although not required, we highly recommend that you use thermal compound to help transfer heat from the processor to the cooler. The Thermaltake Polo 735 comes with a small tube of this stuff. Some motherboard manufacturers will throw some in for you too, but don't count on it; buy some.

Did You Get All of That?

So, what do you think? Do you have a good grip on the basic components you'll need to build your first computer? If not, just give this chapter another quick read—or come back to it and use it as a reference when you need a fast refresher.

We understand that this is a lot of information to tackle the first time around, but it's our hope that you're starting to feel increasingly more confident about building your own PC. And more excited! Never doubt that you can do it. Think about it. Before you read this chapter, could you name all of the parts that fit inside a computer and what they do? You're already more knowledgeable than most people who have used computers their entire lives.

Now that you're familiar with all of the components that make up the guts of a computer, it's time to determine just what type of computer user you really are.

Chapter 3

What Kind of User Are You?

You can't decide what type of Sweet PC you're going to build without first taking a much closer look at what type of computer user you are. To do this, you need to be honest with yourself so that you end up with a PC that does everything you want it to do at a price you can afford.

Bear in mind that the PC of your dreams may be much different than that of your neighbor or your best friend. If you don't play games, don't build a Gamer; if you plan to do a lot of graphic or multimedia work, don't build an Internet Surfer. We think you get the picture; hopefully we haven't thrown you in a big loop. Not to worry, as always, we're here to help.

Finding Your Inner PC

A truly sweet PC is a fine combination of needs and wants. Determine your needs, throw in a few wants, and you wind up with a PC you can call your own. By now, you should be aware of all the parts that make up a PC. This chapter helps you determine what type of computer user you are and how much computer you really *need*.

To determine how much computer you need, first ask yourself what you're going to do with it and how much you're willing to spend. Our goal is to help you build a machine that's tailored to your needs and uses the highest quality parts you can afford.

You see, the Big PC Manufacturers want you to believe that you need one of their cookie cutter computers, one they've put together for you and configured with one goal in mind—pure profit. For them, it's all about the bottom line. Survey the hardware options and upgrades they offer sometime and compare them to what you can build yourself (by reading this book, you'll be able to do just that). You'll quickly see that you're getting more for your money by building your own PC.

Most people purchase a computer without ever taking the time to figure out what they need. The fact is, the options are endless when you're choosing your own components. Until you've built a bunch of computers or done some extensive research, however, you'll probably fit into one of the six categories we outline in this chapter.

So, what are you waiting for? There's never been a better time to get in touch with your inner PC.

Go With the Flow

The average PC user gets on the computer to check email, finish up some office work, and do a little bit of research or online shopping. Is this all you're going to do with your PC, or do you plan on using it for gaming, video editing, or something more? How you plan on using your PC is the single most important factor in deciding what to build, aside from cost, which is also affected by this decision.

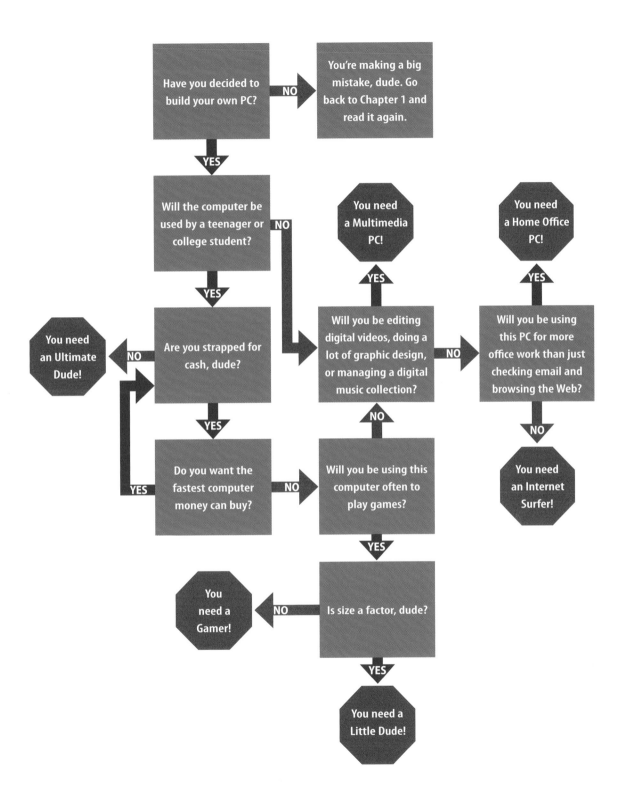

DUDE, This One Time...

We often have friends and family show us their Sunday flyers advertising unbelievably sweet deals on the PCs they want. We try to talk them out of this trap and convince them to build their own PCs, or better yet, let us build the computers for them. Many turn us down because the 3-year warranty, printer, scanner, or free CD burner that gets thrown in to sweeten the pot is too good to pass up.

What ends up happening next? We get phone calls asking, "Hey, why does my computer lock up when my kids try to play this game?" or "Why does my 1-week-old computer restart itself for no reason?" These are just a few examples of what can go wrong. How great is that warranty now? Sure, the Big PC Manufacturers will fix your computer; they may even give you another one. But was your time and frustration worth saving a few bucks? Did that onsite warranty really ease your mind? All that warranty did was sell you a computer that you didn't want to begin with. Take it from us, be your own technical support; build your own sweet PC.

Building the Internet Surfer configuration, for example, costs much less than an Ultimate Dude, but is much more limited in performance.

So, how do you find your inner PC? Just go with the flow. We constructed this flow chart to give you a simple, foolproof method for determining what type of computer you need to build. Start at the top and work your way down to your dream PC.

Find Your Profile

Now that you've found yourself, are you a Little Dude or a Home Office Dude? Or maybe you're a Multimedia Dude? The next step in the process is to skip to the chapter that fits your profile. We created five chapters based on these different profiles that outline exactly what parts to buy to build your ideal system. (You'll find the Internet Surfer configuration in the same chapter as the Home Office PC.) We give you recommendations for specific parts that are based on our years of experience building computers, the price, aesthetics, and user feedback.

After you've read through your list of recommended parts and ordered them, we'll show you step by step how to build a Gamer and a Little Dude. Although we don't have the pages to take you step by step through every configuration, the steps are similar enough that even you Internet Surfer Dudes shouldn't have a problem piecing together your sweet PCs.

Chapter 4

The Home
Office PC

~~~~~~

The Home Office PC is similar to the Internet Surfer (see "The Internet
Surfer" at the end of this chapter) except that it has more juice (**Figure 4.1**).
For this configuration, we double your memory, double your hard drive,
upgrade you to the 64-bit world, and step up to a 17-inch LCD flat panel,
all for the low, low price of around $1,200. Trust us, it's money well spent.
Do a little comparison shopping and you'll see that you can't get a better
off-the-shelf system for the same money.

Figure 4.1: This is a Home Office PC with a 17-inch LCD flat panel, Creative SBS 2.1 350 speakers, and a Logitech LX300 wireless keyboard/mouse combo.

The Home Office PC is designed with business software applications in mind. This PC tower can do everything the Internet Surfer can do—it just does it better and faster because it uses a faster processor and a new motherboard design. With this system, you can open multiple documents and spreadsheets while listening to your favorite CD or streaming audio without skipping a beat.

 **Sweeet!**

If you're happy with the keyboard, mouse, monitor, and speakers that you already have, this system can be built for about $900. That's a great deal for a PC of this caliber!

The Home Office Dude . . .

- ▶ Has a credit card that's not maxed out
- ▶ Is an overachiever who brings his work home
- ▶ Likes to listen to music while he's overachieving
- ▶ Needs a little more horsepower than the Internet Surfer

Table 4.1 shows our recommended component selection for the Home Office PC. You'll quickly notice that we beefed up the memory and ramped up your processing power dramatically. This is a big improvement over the Internet Surfer and should help you power through your busy work efficiently. Don't expect to run the latest 3D games, however, because although we made major upgrades to speed up the Home Office PC, the PowerColor Radeon 9250 video card is effective, but very basic.

Table 4.1: **Home Office System Configuration**	
COMPONENT	RECOMMENDED PRODUCT
Processor	AMD Athlon 64 2800+ (socket 754)
Motherboard	ASUS K8V (socket 754)
Case and power supply	Antec SLK2650-BQE
Memory	512 MB OCZ PC3200 DDR
Video card	PowerColor Radeon 9250
Hard drive	Maxtor 160 GB SATA
Optical drive	Optorite 52×32×52 CD burner
Optical drive	Lite-On IT 16x DVD-ROM
Floppy drive	1.44 MB drive
Sound card	Sound Blaster Live!
Modem card	56 Kbps v.90/92
Operating system	Windows XP Home Edition
Monitor	17-inch LCD flat panel
Input devices	Logitech LX 300
Speakers	Creative SBS 2.1 350

Product listings and prices were accurate at the time this book was published. For the most up-to-date products and prices, please see our Web site at www.dudecomputers.com.

 **Sweeet!**

The best place to view any of the products mentioned in this book and learn more about their specifications is at the respective manufacturers' Web sites. Keep in mind, however, that most manufacturers do not sell directly to the public, and if they do, they usually don't have the best price.

Where's the best place to buy parts? Well, if you're just buying individual parts, we've had good luck with www.newegg.com, www.tigerdirect.com, and www.zipzoomfly.com. Of course, you can always just get one of our pre-configured Dude Kits at www.dude-computers.com and not worry about piecing your computer together or trying to match up parts. If you choose this route, you'll see that we do it all for you—we take the guess work and the headaches out of choosing all the right components—all you have to do is build the thing!

Sweeet!

We love ASUS boards, especially for gamers, but they're a little finicky when it comes to memory, so don't buy generic memory and expect this motherboard to work. This high-class board only works with top-notch memory; we find that ASUS and OCZ make a winning combination.

Components and Software

When designing the Home Office PC, we kept value in mind while we searched for greater performance—a must in the business community. As they say, "time is money," and we don't want you wasting time or losing money because your computer can't handle everything you throw at it. We have to be careful not to get carried away however, because, although a Home Office PC needs to be faster and more powerful than your typical value system, there are areas—such as 3D video—where an office PC doesn't need to excel.

Processor

The AMD Athlon 64 2800+ ($130, www.amd.com) is your processor choice for this system. You may be asking yourself, "AMD processor? Why not Intel?" Or maybe you thought that all computers had an Intel Pentium 4 inside? Well, actually, a lot of them do and there's nothing wrong with those processors. We just like AMD. We like the performance, we like the selection, and we love the price. The AMD Athlon 64 2800+ brings you into the 64-bit world without burning a hole in your wallet. It also equips you to handle all of those 64-bit applications that are due out sometime next year, adding longevity to your system.

Motherboard

We chose the ASUS K8V ($120, www.asus.com) based on months of building with this board. We've experimented with several socket 754 motherboards, and none of them are as stable or as easy to work with. We have yet to witness an ASUS board fail or cause bootup problems.

The ASUS K8V has an accelerated graphics port (AGP) slot for your video card as well as Peripheral Component Interconnect (PCI) slots to spare, even after you install modem and sound cards. The K8V has an onboard large area network (LAN), eight Universal Serial Bus (USB) ports and, of course, controllers for your Serial ATA (SATA) hard drive. Great board, great price.

Case and Power Supply

We picked the all-black Antec SLK2650-BQE ($70, www.antec.com) as our case of choice for the Home Office PC. We prefer black to the traditional beige or two-tones because the PC stays cleaner and looks cooler. You can, of course, choose whatever color you like for the case; we simply recommend our favorites. This case comes with a 350 Watt ATX12V SmartPower power supply, which is also produced by Antec. Trust us when we say that this isn't a cheap power supply like the ones found in other cases within this $70 price range.

Memory

You need at least 512 MB of memory, especially if you work with several windows open at once or need to look at multiple graphics or photos. Memory has a big impact on performance. Check out your local computer shop and compare PCs. You'll notice that the more expensive computers have more memory. Why? Because that super-fast processor won't do you any good if you don't have enough memory to store the processed information. We recommend 512 MB of OCZ PC3200 DDR memory ($80, www.ocztechnology.com). It's a little more expensive than memory sold by other manufacturers, but why quibble over a few bucks when you can get the good stuff this cheap?

Video Card

You can buy the PowerColor Radeon 9250 ($45, www.power-color.com) cheap and it is more than suitable for this rig. Chances are, you won't do any gaming other than the occasional visit to www.playhouse-disney.com or www.nickjr.com, so a high-end card built to support fast 3D graphics is overkill here. The Radeon 9250 produces a beautiful 2D image; you won't be disappointed and the price is just right.

 **Sweeet!**

Want to add a little juice to your Home Office PC without spending too much? For about another $80 you can double your memory from 512 MB to 1 GB. Remember that all data—whether it is coming from your hard drive, the Internet, a digital camera, or the keyboard—has to travel to your memory before it gets to the processor. The more memory you have, the faster your computer performs.

Sweeet!

If you're building a Home Office PC, you're probably bringing work home from your day job. Chances are your boss or coworker may hand you a floppy on your way out the door, so it makes sense to get a floppy drive.

Hard Drive

You need to double the hard drive we recommend in the Internet Surfer, so we suggest you upgrade to a Maxtor 160 GB drive ($100, www.maxtor.com). A 160 GB hard drive provides plenty of storage space for all your office work, plus it leaves enough extra room for your family photos and favorite music.

Optical Drive

In addition to a CD burner, we recommend a DVD player for the Home Office PC. The DVD player lets you watch DVD presentations and movies on your PC and gives you the ability to copy CDs from one drive to another without having to swap CDs or use up hard drive space. We chose the Lite-On IT 16x DVD-ROM ($35, www.liteonit.com), but most DVD drives are of similar quality and they all cost about $30 to $40. If you get the packaged version of this—or any other—optical drive, you may not get the software bundle, which includes a DVD player, so spend the extra couple of bucks and buy your drive retail.

Floppy Drive

Don't be cheap; get yourself a floppy drive. You never know when you may need one and, for as inexpensive as these drives are, it doesn't make sense *not* to get one. If you're looking for suggestions, get a Samsung ($15, www.samsung.com), a Mitsumi ($15, www.mitsumi.com), or a Sony ($15, www.sony.com). Pretty much any floppy drive will do and, as you can see, they all cost about the same.

Sound Card

The Sound Blaster Live! card ($40, www.soundblaster.com)—perfect for the Home Office PC—livens up those value 2.1 speakers we recommend. Sound Blaster cards are manufactured by Creative Labs, which owns most of the home PC market and has a solid reputation for producing cards that pump out excellent audio.

Modem

If your home office can afford to run on dial-up, then go right ahead and get yourself a 56 Kbps modem. Any type and manufacturer will do. The offerings from Creative ($15, www.creative.com), Diamond ($15, www.diamondmm.com) and CNet ($12, www.cnetusa.com) can be had for about $15. Obviously, however, we think that something as important as a business shouldn't have to wait for a slow Internet connection.

Operating System

You'll need to join the rest of the business world and load Windows XP Home Edition ($199, www.windows.com) on your Home Office, especially if your employer uses Windows. Microsoft Windows XP Home Edition owns the home office PC market; it's what everyone else is using and as a result, it's what you need to use.

The major drawback to Windows XP is that it's quite expensive, but you can get it for about half price ($94) by buying the bundled version with your hardware. This version is for system builders like you and doesn't come with manuals or even technical support. All you get is the CD and the license number that allows you to use the product. Don't worry about manuals and technical support though, because we take you through a fresh install of Windows XP in Chapters 9 and 10 ("Building a Gamer" or "Building a Little Dude"). We show you everything you need to know to get Windows running on your machine.

Monitor

A 17-inch LCD flat panel is surprisingly bigger and nicer to look at than a 15-inch flat panel. For home office work, especially if you're pouring over multiple files or windows, you'll need the bigger screen. If a lot of your home office work deals with graphics and/or pictures, you may want to consider an 18-inch or 19-inch flat panel, although these cost a bit more.

We built a computer system for a customer, and not just the computer tower, which is our specialty, but we went the extra mile and picked out the printer, scanner, and digital camera too. We were on a budget, of course, so to save a few dollars, we made some compromises along the way, most notably, we bought a $69 photo printer that had a $20 instant rebate.

Sweet deal for $49, right? Wrong. When we finally got around to installing the system and setting up the printer, we realized that the printer didn't come with any ink cartridges. Turns out that the printer cartridges cost more than the printer! When picking out a printer, find out how much the ink cartridges cost first because that's where printer manufacturers *really* make their money. It's a hidden cost that could end up costing *you* a bundle!

Input Devices

Wireless is the way to go when it comes to picking out a keyboard and a mouse. For the Home Office PC, you'll want to get the Logitech LX 300 wireless combo ($50, www.logitech.com), which allows you to step up to the wireless world of keyboards and mice without burning a huge hole in your wallet. The Logitech Cordless MX Duo ($80, www.logitech.com) is better looking and a little more responsive, but it costs about $30 more. If that's no big deal, go for it; otherwise you'll be fine with this set.

Speakers

These Creative 2.1 speakers fit the bill for your Home Office PC. Creative's SBS 2.1 350 speakers ($40, www.creative.com) sound better than any two-speaker set we've come across in this price range; plus they work well with that Sound Blaster Live! sound card you're building into this rig. Get a set of these and avoid two-speaker sets, your Home Office PC deserves it.

The Internet Surfer

The Internet Surfer is a great PC, albeit the cheapest one we recommend. If you're unsure of what type of PC to build, or are saving up for a Gamer, the Internet Surfer will get you by in style. This PC is also one of the easiest and least intimidating configurations to put together for anyone who is building a computer for the first time.

When we designed the Internet Surfer, value was top priority and quality came in a close second. Our goal is to get you in the game with a stable computer, built with quality parts, at an affordable price. For the money, you can't do better. You can build this system for less than $1,000—pricing fluctuates from week to week, but not by much. If $1,000 is not in your price range, you can use your old monitor, keyboard, mouse, and speakers and build this fast, stable PC tower for closer to $650.

Although most of the components are similar to what you'll need to build the Home Office PC, there are some notable exceptions.

The Processor For the Internet Surfer, you want to get an AMD Sempron processor, which belongs to AMD's newest line of value processors. The AMD Sempron 2400+ ($65, www.amd.com) is not the fastest processor on the market, but it's affordable and, for most tasks, it's amazingly quick. Even though it's a value line processor, don't think for a second that it's not a quality product. It's a deal for the money and should suit your purposes just fine.

Motherboard We chose the ASUS A7V600 ($70, www.asus.com) for this PC. It's stable, affordable, and has integrated LAN (large area network), so you can hook up your broadband Internet connection and a Serial ATA (SATA) controller for your hard drive. It also includes eight Universal Serial Bus (USB) ports, which should be more than enough for your peripheral hardware, including printers, scanners, keyboard, and mouse. It's a great product, despite its low cost.

Memory For this rig, we recommend 256 MB of PC3200 DDR memory from OCZ ($45, www.ocztechnology.com). We prefer OCZ, but you can get your RAM from any reputable memory manufacturer. We thought about going up to 512 MB of RAM for this project, but realized it's not really necessary for the Internet Surfer.

Hard Drive More than 80 GBs of storage for this machine is overkill, but you still want to make sure you buy a quality hard drive. All of your important data is stored on your hard drive, so head off disaster by getting a drive from a manufacturer you can trust. We recommend getting an 80 GB Maxtor drive ($75, www.maxtor.com) for this PC—we like Maxtor and use its drives often.

Monitor We know the Internet Surfer is a value PC, but we recommend spending a few extra bucks for a 15-inch LCD flat panel display instead of a bulky CRT monitor. If you're trying to buy as much screen size as you can afford, keep in mind that a 15-inch flat panel is comparable in viewing area to a 17-inch CRT and it takes up far less space on your desk. If you're really strapped for cash, however, settling on a CRT *can* save you a hundred dollars or so—a cheap 17-inch monitor can cost less than $100.

Chapter 5

The Gamer

All right, here's where we start spending some money (**Figure 5.1**). The Gamer, after all, is a whole different beast than the Internet Surfer or the Home Office PC. You're going to have to pay a little extra for top-of-the-line components, especially when it comes to the processor, memory, and video card. To help you afford these pricier parts, we recommend a smaller hard drive than the one in the Home Office PC and we scale back to just one optical drive.

Figure 5.1: This is a Gamer with a 17-inch LCD flat panel display, Creative's I-Trigue 3400 speakers, and Logitech's Cordless MX Duo keyboard/mouse combo.

 **Sweeet!**

Customization is the name of the game. We tailor our system recommendations to meet your needs, taking into account both performance and price. Our motto? Buy exactly what you need, no more, no less.

The Gamer can play all the latest games and much more. It can burn CDs, edit digital photos and videos, play DVD movies, chug through home office work, and, of course, game all night. This machine can do it all with the exception of high-end digital video editing, which requires a special video card.

How much will all this set you back? How does $1,700 sound? We can even bring that figure down to just $1,150 if you keep your old monitor, mouse, keyboard, and speakers. It's at this level that you start to notice significant savings from building the computer yourself. Shop around, you'll see.

The Gamer Dude . . .

▶ **Needs a fast computer within a reasonable budget**

▶ **Spends a lot of time playing games whether he wins or loses**

▶ **Gives up sleep for the love of the game**

▶ **Is an Ultimate Dude with a salary cap**

Table 5.1 shows our recommended component selection for the Gamer PC. This is the "Best Buy" or "Pound for Pound Champ" of all the PC systems we design and recommend. You get the most processor, video card, and memory for your money at the peak level of performance and price points. In other words, you can get a faster processor, video card, or more memory, but your returns diminish for every dollar above these set price points that you spend. Clear as mud? We hope not, but trust us when we tell you that for the money, this is the best deal out there.

Table 5.1: **Gamer System Configuration**	
COMPONENT	RECOMMENDED PRODUCT
Processor	AMD Athlon 64 3200+ (socket 754)
Motherboard	ASUS K8V (socket 754)
Case and power supply	Antec Sonata
Memory	1,024 MB (1 GB) OCZ PC3200 DDR
Video card	PowerColor Radeon 9800 Pro
Hard drive	Maxtor 80 GB SATA
Optical drive	Lite-On IT 52×32×52×16 DVD-ROM/CD burner combo
Floppy drive	1.44 MB drive
Sound card	Sound Blaster Audigy 2 Value
Modem card	56 Kbps v.90/92
Operating system	Windows XP Home Edition
Monitor	17-inch LCD flat panel
Input devices	Logitech Cordless MX Duo
Speakers	Creative I-Trigue 3400 2.1

Product listings and prices were accurate at the time this book was published. For the most up-to-date products and prices, please see our Web site at www.dudecomputers.com.

 Sweeet!

The three main components that speed up gaming are the processor, memory, and video card, with the video card being slightly more important than the processor, which is slightly more important than memory. This Gamer can hang with the best of them, but remember, you're still gaming on a budget.

 Sweeet!

The best place to view any of the products mentioned in this book and learn more about their specifications is at the respective manufacturers' Web sites. Keep in mind, however, that most manufacturers do not sell directly to the public, and if they do, they usually don't have the best price.

Where's the best place to buy parts? Well, if you're just buying individual parts, we've had good luck with www.newegg.com, www.tigerdirect.com, and www.zipzoomfly.com. Of course, you can always just get one of our pre-configured Dude Kits at www.dude-computers.com and not worry about piecing your computer together or trying to match up parts. If you choose this route, you'll see that we do it all for you—we take the guess work and the headaches out of choosing all the right components—all you have to do is build the thing!

Sweeet!

AMD also makes the Athlon 64 3200+ version with only 512 KB of L2 cache. For gaming, spend the extra $20 and get the 1 MB version. The 512 KB model is a great processor and just as fast, but you never know when that extra cache may come in handy.

Components and Software

When designing the Gamer, we created a machine that keeps up with the latest games without going all out and really tearing into your bank account. The Gamer's processor is a definite step up from the Home Office PC and its memory has doubled to 1,024 MB, or 1 GB. These two upgrades—plus the addition of the PowerColor Radeon 9800 Pro video card—turn the average PC into a serious gaming competitor. We still kept value in mind, however, and got you the best gaming performance for the money. Now, if money is no object, we suggest you skip ahead to Chapter 7 and step up to the Ultimate Dude before you change your mind.

Processor

The Gamer is a speed freak, which is why we recommend the Athlon 64 3200+ processor ($200, www.amd.com). The price is right and it gives your PC enough gas to race through just about any game. This processor also comes with 1 MB of cache, which is twice the cache of the Athlon 64 2800+ (the processor we recommend for the Home Office PC).

You may be asking yourself, "What is cache and why do I need it?" Cache is external memory that resides on the processor and helps it crunch data. Having twice the cache of a typical office PC keeps your processor from getting bogged down while it is processing all the complex 3D graphics that make today's games so fun.

Motherboard

For this system, we're sticking with the ASUS K8V motherboard ($120, www.asus.com), which is the same one we recommend for the Home Office PC. For the money, you can't get a better board. It's rock solid and as stable as can be. As we said before, this board has an accelerated graphics port (AGP) slot for your video card as well as Peripheral Component Interconnect (PCI) slots to spare, even after you install modem and sound cards. The K8V has an onboard large area network (LAN), eight Universal Serial Bus (USB) ports and, of course, controllers for your Serial ATA (SATA) hard drive.

Case and Power Supply

The Antec Sonata ($120, www.antec.com) is an awesome, awesome case. It's a beautiful piano-black case with door covers for the drives and power switch and a neon blue light on the cover that conceals your front audio and USB ports. The power supply is an Antec TruePower 380 watt (True380) power supply that is of much higher quality than the Antec SmartPower (and any other power supply that's included in most cases). This power supply has better cooling, more stable power, and more connectors for all of your internal components. The Sonata is also a dream to work inside. There are very few sharp edges (if any) and it has a roomy design, which is good if you have big hands.

Memory

For gaming, you need more and better memory than you need in other machines. For this configuration, we doubled the RAM to 1,024 MB (1 GB) and stepped up to high-performance DDR that you can buy from high-end memory producers such as OCZ Technology ($225, www.ocztechnology.com). The OCZ PC3200 DDR memory that we're recommending costs about $225 and includes heat spreaders to keep it cool, which is especially important for gaming rigs. No matter what type of memory you get for a Gamer, make sure it has heat spreaders to assist with cooling. And if you're using an ASUS motherboard, don't get cheap "generic" or "house brand" memory or you'll be sorry.

Video Card

The PowerColor Radeon 9800 Pro ($200, www.power-color.com) should be more than enough for the average and above average gamer. It uses the ATI Radeon 9800 Pro graphics processing unit (GPU) and was PowerColor's most expensive video card until the

 **Sweeet!**

We love ASUS boards, especially for gamers, but they're a little finicky when it comes to memory, so don't buy generic memory and expect this motherboard to work. This high-class board only works with top-notch memory; we find that ASUS and OCZ work well together.

Sweeet!

Most games look best at a resolution of 1,280 × 1,024 pixels or higher. If gaming is your thing, make sure your monitor and video card can support these higher resolutions.

release of the new X800 GPU. As dudes on a budget, we personally use this card and love it; the image quality is amazing and the frame rates are super fast.

Hard Drive

We dropped the hard drive down to a Maxtor 80 GB SATA drive ($75, www.maxtor.com) on this PC to free up money better spent on a faster processor, a high-end video card, and extra, faster memory. We're assuming that gaming performance is more critical to you than extra storage space for all of your work files and digital photos. If your Gamer is moonlighting as a Home Office PC, however, we recommend stepping up to a 160 GB drive.

Optical Drive

We like the Lite-On IT 52×32×52×16 DVD-ROM/CD burner combo drive ($40, www.liteonit.com) for the Gamer. The combo drive is basically just a CD burner that can play DVDs as well. We recommend a combo drive for two reasons: to save money and to avoid placing another heat source in your PC. Money and cooling are your big issues in a Gamer, if you haven't already noticed.

Floppy Drive

We advise you to stock this machine with a floppy drive, just in case you ever need one. Plus, floppy drives are cheap enough that cost isn't really an issue. If you need a recommendation, get a Samsung ($15, www.samsung.com), Mitsumi ($15, www.mitsumi.com), or Sony ($15, www.sony.com); any of these will do and, as you can see, they all cost the same.

Sound Card

We can't say enough good things about the Sound Blaster Audigy 2 Value sound card ($50, www.creative.com). It's not Creative's top-of-the-line card, but it brings some of Audigy 2's technology to the game while still keeping the price reasonable enough for us gamers on a budget. This card really brings your games to life and, when combined with the Klipsch ProMedia speakers we recommend, it completely immerses you in your games.

Modem

Don't get one. In fact, don't even think about it. If you plan on doing any online gaming this is not the route for you, my friend. Spend the $40 a month and get yourself a cable modem connection. Contact your local cable TV company for pricing, details, and availability. If you can't get cable modem service, make sure to call your local phone or satellite companies and look into DSL or satellite connections.

Operating System

For the Gamer, you need to install Windows XP Home Edition ($199, www.microsoft.com). The major drawback to Windows XP is that it's quite expensive, but you can get it for about half the price ($94) by buying the bundled version with your hardware. This version is for system builders like you and doesn't come with manuals or even technical support. All you get is the CD and the license number that allows you to use the product. Don't worry about manuals and technical support though, because we take you through a fresh install of Windows XP in Chapters 9 and 10 where we show you how to build a Gamer and a Little Dude. We'll show you everything you need to know to get Windows running on your machine.

Monitor

OK, this is where you can really spend some significant cash, but we're here to say that you won't be sorry if you do. Larger LCD flat panels cost money, but it's money well spent. Get a 17-inch LCD flat panel from a reputable manufacturer, such as Shuttle ($395, www.shuttle.com), ViewSonic ($340, www.viewsonic.com), Samsung ($325, www.samsung.com), or Planar ($300, www.planar.com) and see your games come to life!

 **Sweeet!**

Although there are the rare exceptions, most PC games are designed and written to work with Windows XP. The games that are written for other platforms usually have versions written for Windows XP anyway, so this is your sure-fire bet as far as operating systems go.

 **Sweeet!**

When picking out a flat panel, pay attention to the connection type: either analog or digital. For smaller screen sizes, such as the 15-inch or 17-inch flat panels, you can get away with analog connections. For your more expensive 17-inch and bigger screens, you need to make sure your monitor has a digital video input (DVI) connection, which allows you to see a purely digital picture.

**DUDE,
This One Time...**

We were trying to get a customer in the game. He showed up with flyers from the latest magazines with all kinds of "Gamer" setups, but they were all too expensive for him. He wanted us to build a solid, dependable computer capable of gaming—without the hefty price tag. This was new to us because most gamers that we've worked with in the past didn't consider the budget, they just wanted a machine that would beat the next guy.

We did extensive research on price, performance, and dependability and came up with a parts list that offered the most bang for the buck. Sure, you can spend an extra $50 on an expensive processor, but that doesn't necessarily mean you're going to get an extra $50 worth of performance. The parts we chose for this setup gave our customer the maximum benefit for his dollar. We call this pound for pound champ the "Gamer."

Input Devices

Wireless is the way to go. Logitech sets the bar on quality with the Cordless MX Duo ($75, www.logitech.com). It's more responsive and accurate than other wireless keyboard/mouse combos. If you don't miss fumbling with cables, you won't even be able to tell you've gone wireless!

Speakers

Creative's I-Trigue 3400 speakers ($120, www.creative.com) are a great set of 2.1 speakers—only topped by the Klipsch Pro Media that we recommend for the Multimedia PC and the Ultimate Dude. These I-Trigue speakers, which produce crystal clear highs and heart-pounding lows, save you $20 to $30 over similar systems offered by Klipsch (ProMedia GMX-A, $140) and Altec Lansing (MX 5021, $150).

We have to say, Klipsch ProMedias are hands-down the best 2.1 speaker systems we've ever laid ears on. We place great emphasis on sound and for good reason—good speakers allow you to experience the game, not just hear it! But if you're eager to get in the game and still save some money, you can't go wrong with this set of Creative I-Trigue 3400 speakers.

Chapter 6

The Multimedia PC

The Multimedia PC is a jack-of-all-trades with a specialty in one: digital video (**Figure 6.1**). For this bad boy, we threw in an ATI video card that has a built-in TV tuner and digital video input (DVI) so that you can download digital video straight from your camcorder. We also upped the storage space with a 200 GB hard drive and included a DVD burner. If you plan on using your PC for everything from editing photos to shopping online, this is the build for you.

Figure 6.1: This is a Multimedia PC with a 17-inch LCD flat panel display, Klipsch ProMedia GMX A-2.1 speakers, and Logitech's Cordless MX Duo keyboard/mouse combo.

 **Sweeet!**

If you've already got peripherals that you like and want to keep, keep 'em and save yourself some money. You can build the PC without peripherals for about $1,300.

The Multimedia PC can do everything well, except play tech-heavy, graphic-intensive games. That doesn't mean you can't use it for gaming. You *can*, you just won't get the best possible performance from those games where the people look more realistic than you do. If that's what you really want, go back and build a Gamer.

You can, however, use the Multimedia PC to convert those old VHS tapes to digital video, edit home movies and burn them to DVD, and easily zip through any office or school work. You can even use it to watch TV. We recommend this system frequently because it allows you to do so much for just $1,800. You'll have a hard time finding a system this good for a price this low anywhere—it's an entertainment package and a PC all rolled into one.

The Multimedia Dude . . .

▶ **Likes being able to do a little bit of everything**

▶ **Plays the occasional game, but quits when he loses**

▶ **Spends hours converting those VHS tapes to DVD format**

▶ **Is susceptible to having numerous and fancy peripherals**

Table 6.1 shows our recommended component selection for the Multimedia PC. With this machine, we were looking for a little more processing power and a lot more flexibility in the graphics department. We were careful to choose a video card with inputs that enable you to connect analog devices—such as VCRs, camcorders, and TVs—to your PC. The card also has a graphics processing unit (GPU) powerful enough to convert analog files into digital ones.

Working with video files consumes a lot of memory and hard drive space, so we've provided plenty of each in this configuration. And, of course, we topped things off with a DVD player and a dual-layer DVD burner. You'll want to get a dual-layer DVD burner because it burns twice as much data (9.4 GB) as a single layer DVD burner.

 **Sweeet!**

The best place to view any of the products mentioned in this book and learn more about their specifications is at the respective manufacturers' Web sites. Keep in mind, however, that most manufacturers do not sell directly to the public, and if they do, they usually don't have the best price.

Where's the best place to buy parts? Well, if you're just buying individual parts, we've had good luck with www.newegg.com, www.tigerdirect.com, and www.zipzoomfly.com. Of course, you can always just get one of our pre-configured Dude Kits at www.dude-computers.com and not worry about piecing your computer together or trying to match up parts. If you choose this route, you'll see that we do it all for you—we take the guess work and the headaches out of choosing all the right components—all you have to do is build the thing!

Table 6.1: Multimedia System Configuration

COMPONENT	RECOMMENDED PRODUCT
Processor	AMD Athlon 64 3400+ (socket 939)
Motherboard	ASUS A8V Deluxe (socket 939)
Case and power supply	Antec Sonata with 380 watt TruePower power supply
Memory	1,024 MB OCZ PC3200 DDR
Video card	ATI All-In-Wonder Radeon 9600
Hard drive	Maxtor 200 GB 7.200 rpm
Optical drive	Toshiba 16x DVD-ROM
Optical drive	Optorite 16x dual-layer DVD burner
Floppy drive	1.44 MB drive
Sound card	Sound Blaster Audigy 2 Value
Modem card	Not required
Operating system	Windows XP Home Edition
Monitor	17-inch LCD flat panel
Input devices	Logitech Cordless MX Duo
Speakers	Klipsch ProMedia GMX A-2.1

Product listings and prices were accurate at the time this book was published. For the most up-to-date products and prices, please see our Web site at www.dudecomputers.com.

Sweeet!

This processor has a socket 939, so don't make the mistake of picking up a socket 754 motherboard for the AMD 64-bit processors.

Sweeet!

Don't get tempted into buying a cheap motherboard to save a few bucks—you will regret it. We've built with many boards other than ASUS, but we got tired of the problems, confusion, and inevitable returns. If you want this build to go as smoothly as possible, use the boards we recommend—they've worked great for us and can work great for you, too! If you can't get your hands on an ASUS board, you'll find that EPoX and MSI make excellent boards as well. We've had good luck with them both.

Components and Software

When we got ready to design the Multimedia PC, we set out to create a machine that could do it all for just $2,000. Surprisingly, we got all this performance for a couple of hundred dollars less. We told you we could save you money! Of course, when you compare this PC to an off-the-shelf model, you'll notice that the savings are even greater.

Processor

For this build, we recommend the AMD Athlon 64 3400+ processor ($240, www.amd.com). Although we chose the 512 KB cache model to save you about $40, this processor is still faster than the Athlon 64 3200+. Trust us, you need the extra speed to get through those large video files. If you're worried you won't have *enough* speed—because you think you're Martin Scorsese or something—keep in mind that *we're* keeping *your* budget in mind. The next step up in processors will set you back a couple of hundred dollars, which is why we recommend that you stick with the 3400+. It's fast. Well, it's fast enough, anyway.

Motherboard

We chose the ASUS A8V Deluxe ($140, www.asus.com) for this system. This is a great motherboard with plenty of Peripheral Component Interconnect (PCI) slots, an accelerated graphics port (AGP) slot for your sweet video card, an integrated large area network (LAN) connection, and lots of Universal Serial Bus (USB) ports for all the fancy peripherals you need for your digital studio. This board is similar in features to all the previously mentioned boards; the only difference is that it supports the socket 939 design.

Case and Power Supply

The Antec Sonata ($120, www.antec.com) is our favorite case and we use it for most of our builds. If you've read the previous chapters, you know that we recommend it a lot. How could we not? It's a beautiful, piano black case with door covers for the drives and power switch, and a neon blue light on the cover that conceals your front audio and USB ports. The convenient location of the USB ports makes it easy to plug in digital video camcorders and digital cameras—perfect for the Multimedia PC. The Sonata is also fun and easy to build with because it has a spacious interior with few, if any, sharp edges.

The Sonata's power supply is an Antec TruePower 380 watt power supply that is of much higher quality than the power supplies included in most other cases.

Memory

You'll need to fortify your Multimedia PC with 1 GB of memory to handle all those large, digital video files. You won't, however, need the fancy schmancy memory we recommend for the Gamer, so pick up 1 GB OCZ PC3200 ($170, www.ocztechnology.com). Heat spreaders aren't as critical for this system, so you can save some cash and equip this rig with standard DDR memory from a reputable manufacturer, such as OCZ Technology.

Video Card

The ATI All-In-Wonder Radeon 9600 video card ($175, www.ati.com) comes with a built-in TV tuner, which means you can run your cable or satellite TV through it and watch TV at your desk. This awesome card also lets you play most games and can handle any digital video or digital photography task you throw at it. Such an all-round work-horse is the perfect choice for the Multimedia PC.

Sweeet!

ASUS boards are a little finicky when it comes to memory, so don't buy generic memory and expect this motherboard to work. This high-class board only works with top-notch memory; we find that ASUS and OCZ work well together.

Sweeet!

There are other vendors that offer the All-In-Wonder cards using ATI GPUs, but we stick with ATI because the software that it bundles with its All-In-Wonder cards is very useful. This software bundle makes converting old VHS tapes, editing digital video, and viewing the final product a breeze.

If you're planning on doing some serious gaming with this PC—in addition to everything else—you might want to step up to the ATI All-In-Wonder Radeon 9800 Pro card ($280). Those of you with an eye on the budget should know, however, that this card adds significantly to the cost of the machine.

Hard Drive

You're going to need a lot of storage space, and the Maxtor 200 GB SATA drive ($150, www.maxtor.com) provides just that, lots of space. After all, if you're working with big digital video files, you've got to store it somewhere, and this drive delivers. If you can't get a Maxtor drive, get a 200 GB SATA drive from Western Digital or Seagate. They make great products too, we just happen to prefer Maxtor from years of using its products successfully.

Optical Drives

Toshiba is a quality drive manufacturer, and the Toshiba 16x DVD-ROM ($35, www.toshiba.com) is a reliable drive that lasts forever. We don't recommend installing a CD-ROM drive in this case because it takes away from the system's flexibility. Yeah, you could save $15, but we don't think it's worth it. Spend a few extra bucks and give yourself the ability to play DVDs instead. Seriously, when was the last time anyone released a movie you could watch on a CD-ROM?

This Optorite 16x dual-layer DVD burner ($90, www.optorite.com) is also a nice drive. It's fast, solid, and has quality written all over it. That's not to say that other drives won't compare, but we've personally built systems with this drive and can say we like it. Like other DVD burners, this one can write data to CDs as well. The dual-layer 16x DVD is key because it allows you to store 9.4 GB of data on a single DVD rather than 4.7 GB if you had a single-layer DVD burner. It's only an additional $20 to get a dual-layer DVD burner over a single-layer one, so why not upgrade?

Floppy Drive

We advise you to stock this machine with a floppy drive, just in case you ever need one. Plus, floppy drives are cheap enough that cost isn't really an issue. If you need a recommendation, get a Samsung ($15, www.samsung.com), Mitsumi ($15, www.mitsumi.com), or Sony ($15, www.sony.com); any of these will do and, as you can see, they all cost about the same.

Sound Card

With the Sound Blaster Audigy 2 Value card ($50, www.creative.com), you'll be able to use this PC to run your entire entertainment system. This card provides crystal clear highs and booming lows and it works well with the Klipsch speakers that we recommend for this system.

Modem

Not required. Enough said. You didn't think we'd leave you with that did you? Seriously, if you're spending this much money and building a machine of this caliber, you should invest in high-speed Internet service, such as a cable modem or DSL. We understand that some areas don't offer this type of service; if that's the case, you may want to consider satellite Internet service.

If satellite service is out of the question and it's dialing up through a modem or nothing, get a v.92 modem card from any manufacturer, but don't spend too much money. Modem cards range from $6 to $70. The last one we purchased from a local computer shop cost about $10 and it worked just fine. Some of the modem card manufacturers we've had luck with in the past include Creative (www.creative.com), CNet (www.cnetusa.com), and Diamond (www.diamondmm.com).

Sweeet!

Be wary of the flat panel that is much cheaper than most others. If it sounds too cheap to be true, it is.

Sweeet!

These days, the sound blasting out of your computer speakers can rival anything that comes from a high-end home audio system. Computer speakers now range from 2.1 setups all the way to 7.1 surround sound. For those of you who aren't home audio aficionados—yet—a 2.1 setup means you have a total of three speakers in your system, two satellite speakers, and a subwoofer. A speaker system that is 7.1 has eight speakers, seven satellites (for ultimate surround sound) and one subwoofer. If you haven't caught on yet, the .1 accounts for the subwoofer, which helps fill in the low-end, earth shaking boom.

Operating System

You really don't have much choice here. For this PC, as with the others, you need to install Windows XP Home Edition ($199, www. microsoft.com). The major drawback to Windows XP is that it's quite expensive, but you can get it for about half the price ($94) by buying the bundled version with your hardware. This version is for system builders like you and doesn't come with manuals or even technical support. All you get is the CD and the license number that allows you to use the product. Don't worry about manuals and technical support though, because we take you through a fresh install of Windows XP in Chapters 9 and 10 ("Building a Gamer" and "Building a Little Dude"). In both of these chapters, we show you everything you need to know to get Windows running on your machine.

Monitor

You'll want to get a 17-inch LCD flat panel to trick out this system. Go with a reputable manufacturer and make sure it has DVI connections to your PC. We've tested monitors that have both digital and analog connections and, as expected, the picture was much nicer when we used the digital connection. We like the 17-inch LCD flat panel offers from Shuttle ($395, www.shuttle.com), ViewSonic ($340, www.viewsonic.com), Samsung ($325, www.samsung.com), or Planar ($300, www.planar.com). You can't go wrong when you buy quality.

Input Devices

The Logitech Cordless MX Duo ($75, www.logitech.com) is once again the wireless keyboard and mouse combination of choice, even for the Multimedia PC. It looks cool, the keys are soft, the mouse is responsive, there are no messy wires, and it's pretty affordable, considering what you get.

Speakers

Once again, we recommend the Klipsch ProMedia GMX A-2.1 ($140, www.klipsch.com) speaker setup. This is another one of our favorite components, and for good reason. You've got to take our word on it for this one, but these speakers are unbelievable. They can fill your entire house with clear, rich sound and a deep, full bass—simple as that. Nothing complements an awesome PC like a killer set of Klipsch.

DUDE, This One Time...

Back when SATA drives were relatively new, we bulk ordered parts for six computers that needed to be finished and delivered to our customers by December 24th. It was our holiday rush and we were set to make a pretty hefty profit. Everything was going great, until the parts showed up.

We got our SATA drives, only to realize that the motherboards didn't have SATA controllers and couldn't support the drives. We went on a parts run to three different shops to get new motherboards with SATA controllers. That little fiasco cost us 24 hours of time and about $600 in profit—parts are much more expensive to buy retail than on the Internet. So, instead of wrapping gifts and trimming our Christmas trees, we spent the last few days before Christmas building computers. Lesson learned? Read the specs and always make sure that all of your parts are compatible *before* you order them.

Chapter 7

The Ultimate Dude

If you thought the Gamer was an expensive and powerful machine, it's nothing compared to the Ultimate Dude (**Figure 7.1**). This is the fastest computer we could design for you and still keep the cost right at $3,000. You heard us right: $3,000. This machine is a beast. It eats up anything you throw at it; that $4,300 high-end Dell doesn't even come close to this thing.

We handpicked every component in this PC to bring you the ultimate gaming experience. Although not every component is the best money can buy, they don't all need to be. That's the beauty of building your own system. A similar off-the-shelf system would cost you about $1,000 more (and we're being conservative here) and would force you to foot the bill for components you just don't need. Are you excited about this? You should be! We love the Ultimate Dude!

Figure 7.1: This is an Ultimate Dude with a 19-inch LCD flat panel, Klipsch ProMedia GMX A-2.1 speakers, and wireless Gyration Ultra GT keyboard and mouse combo.

What can the Ultimate Dude do? We think it's faster to tell you what it *can't* do. The Ultimate Dude's video card is purely for gaming, so it lacks the connections and bundled software that come with the Multimedia PC's ATI All-In-Wonder Radeon card. As a result, you won't be able to connect analog devices, such as camcorders, to your Ultimate Dude, which means you won't be able to convert VHS tapes into digital video, as you can with the Multimedia PC. You can also forget about using this dude as a replacement for your TV. But that's it for the no-can-dos. This slammin' PC can handle anything else you throw at it.

In fact, this PC is so fast that it seems to anticipate your every move, opening Web pages almost before you finish typing in the URL or pulling the trigger in the latest 3D shoot-'em-up before you've fired the virtual gun. And, not only does it work well, but it sounds great. The Klipsch ProMedia GMX A-2.1 speaker set paired with the Sound Blaster Audigy 2 ZS sound card makes a wicked combination that will certainly replace many home audio systems out there.

Figure 7.1 shows the recommended components for the Ultimate Dude and, let us be the first to say, this rig is high tech. We hand-picked every component and only the best passed the test. The Antec case is a thing of beauty, as is the Thermaltake central processing unit

(CPU) cooler. All of these high-end components need a lot of juice, however, which is why we've thrown in the Antec NeoPower 480 watt power supply.

The Ultimate Dude . . .

- ▶ Is even more addicted to gaming than the Gamer
- ▶ Believes money is no object when it comes to building the perfect PC
- ▶ Upgrades often, whether he needs to or not
- ▶ Plays to win

Table 7.1: Ultimate Dude System Configuration

COMPONENT	RECOMMENDED PRODUCT
Processor	AMD Athlon 64 FX (socket 939)
Heat sink and fan	Thermaltake Polo 735 (aftermarket cooler)
Motherboard	ASUS A8V Deluxe (socket 939)
Case	Antec P160
Power Supply	Antec NeoPower 480 watt
Memory	1 GB OCZ High Performance PC3200 DDR
Video card	PowerColor Radeon X800 Pro
Hard drive	Western Digital Raptor 74 GB SATA
Optical drive	Lite-On IT 16x DVD-ROM
Optical drive	Optorite Dual Layer 16x DVD Burner
Floppy drive	None required
Sound card	Sound Blaster Audigy 2 ZS
Modem card	Not required
Operating system	Windows XP Home Edition
Monitor	19-inch LCD flat panel
Input devices	Gyration Ultra GT keyboard and mouse combo
Speakers	Klipsch ProMedia GMX A-2.1

Product listings and prices were accurate at the time this book was published. For the most up-to-date products and prices, please see our Web site at www. dudecomputers.com.

 **Sweeet!**

The best place to view any of the products mentioned in this book and learn more about their specifications is at the respective manufacturers' Web sites. Keep in mind, however, that most manufacturers do not sell directly to the public, and if they do, they usually don't have the best price.

Where's the best place to buy parts? Well, if you're just buying individual parts, we've had good luck with www.newegg.com, www.tigerdirect. com, and www.zipzoomfly.com. Of course, you can always just get one of our preconfigured Dude Kits at www.dudecomputers.com and not worry about piecing your computer together or trying to match up parts. If you choose this route, you'll see that we do it all for you—we take the guess work and the headaches out of choosing all the right components— all you have to do is build the thing!

 **Sweeet!**

Don't forget to install the fan controller that comes with the Polo 735 aftermarket cooler. If you do not install the controller, this cooler sounds like a helicopter hovering over your house. This thing is loud because it's designed for maximum cooling; the controller allows the fan to run much slower when the processor isn't so hot.

 *DUDE, This One Time...*

A good buddy of ours dropped an Athlon 64 FX processor while building his Ultimate Dude. Do you know what a brand new $800 processor with bent pins looks like? We do, and it isn't pretty. Neither was the look on our friend's face as he stood there holding his useless, bent processor. The moral of this story? When you shell out close to $2,500 in parts to build an Ultimate Dude, treat those parts with care. They are sturdy, but when one of those processors hits the ground, pins get bent and bad things happen.

Components and Software

When we designed the Ultimate Dude, we were pretty excited about building and using such an elegant beast. To be honest, this isn't something—like sky diving or coffee with Scarlett Johansson—that we get to do very often. Most people don't build a machine with this type of processing power and most users (about 90 percent) don't need it. It's incredibly fast, but it costs a lot of money and produces a sweltering amount of heat.

To keep this rig within the realm of possibility for hard-core gamers, we tried to stay within a $3,000 budget and were able to meet that goal without sacrificing any performance. We also managed to keep the heat down with a very efficient and reliable power supply, an aluminum case with cooling fans, and a Thermaltake aftermarket processor cooler. As a finishing touch, we maxed out the speed on this racehorse by giving it AMD's fastest processor, ATI's fastest video card, high performance memory from OCZ, and Western Digital's Raptor hard drive, which spins at 10,000 rpm versus the more standard drives that turn at a mere 7,200 rpm.

Processor

To do this system justice, we couldn't settle for anything less than AMD's best—the AMD Athlon 64 FX ($800, www.amd.com). All we can say about this processor is, Wow! This little number cruncher is smokin' fast—no other processor on the market even comes close to keeping up with it.

It can get hot though, especially under a heavy load, which is why we chose an aftermarket processor cooler to keep it from burning up. The Polo 735 ($40, www.thermaltake.com) from Thermaltake is sturdy, quiet, and effective. It adds to the price of your processor, but when you're spending this kind of money, another $40 is nothing.

Motherboard

We chose the ASUS A8V Deluxe ($140, www.asus.com) for this rig because it's stable, fast, and comes from a respected manufacturer. This board has all the slots and connectors you need, including five Peripheral Component Interconnect (PCI) slots, eight Universal Serial Bus (USB) connections, four Serial ATA (SATA) controllers, and the all-important large area network (LAN) connection for that high-speed Internet connection that serves as your portal to the online gaming community. This motherboard also has two IEEE-1394 or FireWire connections, which allow you to transfer data quickly (400 to 800 Mbps) from your digital camcorder or camera to your PC.

Case and Power Supply

The Ultimate Dude is no ordinary computer—it's got needs. Because it generates so much heat and noise, we took extra measures with the case and chose the Antec P160 ($150, www.antec.com), a stunning silver case constructed entirely of anodized aluminum, which releases heat much better than steel. It also comes with built-in ball bearing fans that are quiet and also help reduce heat.

The case is as beautiful as it is functional, with a clear side panel for your viewing pleasure. The only disadvantage to its see-through sides is that now you have to be very neat with how you route your cables—although you should really be doing that anyway to keep tangled cables from blocking airflow.

For power, we went with the rugged Antec NeoPower 480 watt power supply ($135, www.antec.com). This power supply has a reputation for putting out very stable and reliable power, plus it comes with built-in noise-reduction features.

 **Sweeet!**

We love ASUS boards, especially for high-end builds like the Ultimate Dude, but they're a little finicky when it comes to memory, so don't buy generic memory and expect this motherboard to work. This high-class board only works with top-notch memory; we find that ASUS and OCZ make a winning combination.

Sweeet!

Your video card must support your monitor's screen resolution and vice versa. If your monitor can support a higher resolution than your video card, then your video card is your limiting factor, and vice versa. For example, let's say that you purchased a Compaq PC last year and it came with a 17-inch CRT monitor. Now, you want to upgrade to a flat panel, so you go out and buy a Planar 19-inch LCD flat panel. You open the box, hook up the monitor, and notice that the colors are weird and the screen looks blurry.

What the heck happened?

Your PC probably uses onboard video or some sort of super cheap video card that doesn't support the higher resolutions your monitor requires. Chances are, you'll also need to upgrade your video card before you can get the most out of your new computer screen.

Memory

As with the original Gamer, we recommend 1 GB of OCZ High Performance memory ($225, www.ocztechnology.com) for this rig. This memory is designed to perform faster than standard PC3200 DDR and has built-in heat spreaders to help dissipate heat evenly, keeping your memory fast and cool. Containing heat is important when you're building any gaming rig, so always make sure your memory has heat spreaders. You know what happens when your memory gets hot, right? Your computer can grind to a near halt or, even worse, shut down and never start back up again.

If you really want this baby to fly, go ahead and bump up your memory to 2 GB, but brace yourself for the $300 price jump that comes with it.

Video Card

The PowerColor Radeon X800 Pro ($475, www.power-color.com) is now one of PowerColor's top-of-the line video cards, replacing the Radeon 9800 Pro series. There is a Radeon X800 XT model that costs a couple of hundred dollars more, but we don't feel it's worth the extra outlay of cash; you probably wouldn't notice a difference in performance between the two anyway.

The PowerColor Radeon X800 Pro is amazing. The images are pristine, the frame rates are super fast, and the bundled software includes an aftermarket DVD player, digital media software, backup software, production software, director software, and two games: Hitman and Counter Strike.

Hard Drive

You're probably wondering why we dropped the storage space from 80 GB, which we recommend in other systems, to 74 GB. Well, we really didn't have a choice. For the previous systems we've outlined in this book, we recommended 7,200 rpm drives, which work well for those systems. For the Ultimate Dude, however, we step up to the 10,000 rpm Western Digital Raptor ($190, www.westerndigital.com), which is much quicker, despite the fact that storage space on this speed demon currently caps out at 74 GB. It's an excellent drive though, and it *is* noticeably faster. It's definitely worth the money to have this speed and be the first on your network connection to run at 10,000 rpm.

Optical Drive

As far as optical drives go, we chose a setup similar to that of the Multimedia PC. We recommend a 16x DVD-ROM from Lite-On IT ($30, www.liteonit.com) and a dual layer 16x DVD burner from Optorite ($90, www.optorite.com). The dual layer 16x DVD is key because it allows you to store 9.4 GB of data on one DVD, whereas a single layer DVD burner only lets you store 4.7 GB of data per DVD. The dual layer DVD burner only costs about $20 more than a single layer burner, so it just makes sense to upgrade, especially when you're already investing this much money to create a top-of-the-line PC.

Floppy Drive

We hate to go against everything we've said in the past, but you don't need a stinking floppy for this PC. The components in this rig already produce a lot of heat, so you're better off *not* adding another heat source. One less component also leaves more room in the case for air to circulate, which helps to cool off the other components.

Instead of a floppy, we suggest investing in a 512 MB flash drive, such as a SanDisk Cruzer Mini ($50, www.sandisk.com) or a Lexar JumpDrive ($50, www.lexar.com). A flash drive, which can also be called a *jump drive* or *memory stick,* is a memory device that plugs into your USB port for external data storage. A flash drive serves the same purpose as a floppy, but holds much more data, is very small and stable, and looks way cooler.

Sweeet!

If you're concerned about someone handing you a floppy on your way out of the office or classroom, don't worry. These USB flash drives plug easily into your computer and require no setup, they just work. Transferring files from a floppy or an email attachment is quick and easy, you just insert the floppy, copy the file, and paste it onto your USB drive folder. Doesn't get easier than that. We couldn't imagine working without these drives—they're the most useful tools we've ever come across, other than the PC itself.

Sound Card

If you liked the Sound Blaster Audigy 2 Value sound card—which we recommend for the less expensive configurations—you haven't heard anything yet. For the Ultimate Dude, we recommend the Audigy 2 ZS ($100, www.creative.com), which blows the value card out of the water in terms of performance.

The Audigy 2 ZS, for example, has a signal-to-noise ratio of 108 decibels (dB), a max sampling rate of 192 KHz, analog and digital out connections, and one IEEE-1394 FireWire connection, which incorporates Dolby Digital EX. The value card, on the other hand, has a signal-to-noise ratio of just 100 dB, a max sampling rate of 96 KHz, and only offers analog out connections.

What does all this mean to you? Simply that the Audigy 2 ZS is a strata above the Audigy 2 Value (or the Live!) sound card and that it produces louder sound (with minimal distortion at high volumes) and audio that's clearer and crisper at all volumes and frequencies. Combine this sound card with the Klipsch ProMedia speakers—or any high-end 2.1 speaker system—and you'll definitely have enough quality to replace many home audio systems.

Audiophiles should know that the Audigy 2 ZS isn't the most expensive card that Creative sells. Creative also produces an Audigy 4 sound card ($300, www.creative.com), but we're not recommending that card for this machine because we feel it's not worth the money unless you're setting up a 7.1 speaker system. If you *are* setting up a 7.1 audio system, by all means, spend the extra cash and get the Audigy 4—it gives you much greater control over each individual speaker.

Modem

If you're spending this kind of money and building a machine as powerful as this one, you should invest in high-speed Internet service, such as a cable modem or DSL. We understand that some areas don't offer this type of service, so if you live in one of these areas, you may want to consider satellite Internet service. But if paying upwards of $60 a month (plus a huge initial setup fee) for satellite service is not in your budget, then buy a modem as a last resort.

You can get a v.92 modem card from any manufacturer, but don't spend too much money. Modem cards range from $6 to $70. The last one we purchased from a local computer shop cost about $10 and it worked just fine. Some of the modem card manufacturers we've had luck with in the past include Creative (www.creative.com), CNet (www.cnetusa.com), and Diamond (www.diamondmm.com).

Operating System

For this PC, as with the others described in this book, you'll need to install Windows XP Home Edition ($199, www.windows.com). The major drawback to Windows XP is that it's quite expensive, but you can get it for about half the price ($94) by buying the bundled version with your hardware. This version is for system builders like you and doesn't come with manuals or even technical support. All you get is the CD and the license number that allows you to use the product. Don't worry about manuals and technical support though, because we take you through a fresh install of Windows XP in Chapters 9 and 10 and show you everything you need to know to get Windows running on your machine.

Monitor

Yes, 19-inch LCD flat panel monitors are expensive, but going with anything smaller would be a terrible injustice—not just to your video card—but to your entire setup. A gorgeous, 19-inch LCD flat panel, combined with the high-resolution capabilities and processing power of the PowerColor Radeon X800 Pro video card, brings the latest 3D games to life.

Don't be cheap—get the good stuff and buy your monitor from a reputable manufacturer. If you want quality without paying astronomical prices, we recommend the Planar PE1900 ($390, www.planar.com) or the ViewSonic VG900b ($400, www.viewsonic.com). If you're willing to spend a little extra for premium image quality, stick with the Samsung 910T ($475, www.samsung.com) or the ViewSonic VP191b ($500, www.viewsonic.com).

As always, do your research before buying anything. Some good places to start for monitors are www.pcworld.com, www.pcmag.com, or even www.consumerreports.com (subscription required). And, of course, we're constantly doing our research and trying out new products, so you can always visit our Web site at www.dudecomputers.com to see which monitors we're currently recommending.

Sweeet!

Power output is rated in watts and you want as much of it as will fit in your budget. The more power output you have, the cleaner and louder your speakers will sound. For a three-piece setup (2.1 sound), you need at least 30 watts to get nice sound. Lower-end systems average about 10 watts of power and tend to distort your audio when you turn up the volume. The middle ground is about 30 watts, while the audiophile setups are normally 50 watts and higher and well worth the price.

Input Devices

For this high class rig, we take it up a notch. The wireless Gyration Ultra GT ($110, www.gyration.com) keyboard and mouse combo is nothing short of excellent. The keyboard boasts an additional 15 hot keys, some of which you can program to do things like access the Internet, increase the volume, play a CD and skip through songs, conduct a search, or even check email.

This well-designed keyboard has some of the softest keys we've come across and the mouse is even more responsive than the one included with the Logitech MX Duo. This mouse even works in midair! That's right—no table required. Just press the trigger finger button and move the mouse around, then let go when the cursor is where you want it. We love this feature and use this mouse at work when we're giving slide presentations.

Speakers

If you're an Ultimate dude, you need the ultimate speakers. Klipsch ProMedia GMX A-2.1 speakers ($140, www.klipsch.com) are expensive, but they're the best we've heard. When we went looking for the best high-end speakers, we did what any consumer would do. We went to our local computer and electronic stores and listened to every set they had on display—*not* a fast process. We then bought the three sets that sounded the best—the Creative I-Trigue 3400, the Klipsch ProMedia GMX A, and the Altec Lansing MX5021.

These speakers are all high-end and cost about the same when you're shopping online, from $130 to $150. We've owned them for a couple of months now and have come to the conclusion that the Klipsch ProMedia GMX A-2.1 setup is just a bit better than the other two sets. The tweeters produce crisper highs (almost screeching); the mid speakers produce better vocals, guitars, and pianos; and the subwoofer's thunderous boom is actually so powerful that most of the time we only keep it turned halfway up. We recommend that you try a set for yourself. We think you'll agree that these speakers, quite literally, rock.

Chapter 8

The Little Dude

A cross between the Gamer and the Ultimate Dude, the Little Dude
is proof that good things do come in small packages (**Figure 8.1**).
Portable and powerful, the Little Dude looks sharp in a Small Form
Factor (SFF) case from Shuttle that's well designed, durable, and features
an innovative heat sink/radiator central processing unit (CPU) cooler
codenamed ICE (Integrated Cooling Engine). Of course, no PC is perfect—with its small size come certain drawbacks—but the Little Dude
packs a lot of performance in a compact case and is an absolute breeze
to build.

Figure 8.1: This is a Little Dude with a Shuttle XP17 17-inch portable LCD display, Altec Lansing VS2120 2.0 speakers, and Logitech Cordless MX Duo wireless keyboard/mouse combo.

The Little Dude can do everything the Gamer can do—play games, burn CD compilations, do office and school work, edit digital photos . . . you name it. In fact, the Little Dude is built with slightly more processing power than the Gamer to offer you a middle ground between the Gamer and the Ultimate Dude. Plus, it's portable! Unlike any of the other PCs we tell you about in this book, the Little Dude can travel with you anywhere and costs just $1,200 to build—$1,700 if you include all the fun peripherals.

Table 8.1 shows the recommended components for this PC. You may notice that we didn't recommend a motherboard and we *did* recommend a two-speaker setup, which we said we'd never do. Let us explain. The Shuttle SFF case comes with a motherboard specifically designed for it and the low-end speakers are only for when you're on the road and need portability. We also recommend a set of high-end speakers for when this Little Dude is *not* on tour. This rig is very similar to the Gamer, with the exception of the upgraded processor and the downgraded audio capabilities. One makes up for the other; any compromises or shortcomings were all hard decisions we had to make due to size and heat constraints. Let's get to the details, shall we?

The Little Dude . . .

▶ Believes that smaller is better

▶ Wants to build a powerful PC fast

▶ Is a regular attendee at your local LAN party

▶ Does not leave home without it—the PC, that is

Table 8.1: **Little Dude System Configuration**

COMPONENT	RECOMMENDED PRODUCT
Processor	AMD Athlon 64 3400+ (socket 754)
Small Form Factor bare-bones system	Shuttle XPC SN85G4 (socket 754)
Memory	1 GB High Performance OCZ PC3200 DDR
Video card	PowerColor Radeon 9800 Pro
Hard drive	Maxtor 80 GB SATA
Optical drive	Optorite 16x dual layer DVD burner
Sound card	Integrated
Modem	Not recommended
Operating system	Windows XP Home Edition
Monitor	Shuttle XP17 17-inch portable LCD
Input devices	Logitech Cordless MX Duo
Speakers	Altec Lansing VS2120

Product listings and prices were accurate at the time this book was published. For the most up-to-date products and prices, please see our Web site at www. dudecomputers.com.

 **Sweeet!**

The best place to view any of the products mentioned in this book and learn more about their specifications is at the respective manufacturers' Web sites. Keep in mind, however, that most manufacturers do not sell directly to the public, and if they do, they usually don't have the best price.

Where's the best place to buy parts? Well, if you're just buying individual parts, we've had good luck with www. newegg.com, www.tigerdirect.com, and www.zipzoomfly.com. Of course, you can always just get one of our preconfigured Dude Kits at www. dudecomputers.com and not worry about piecing your computer together or trying to match up parts. If you choose this route, you'll see that we do it all for you—we take the guess work and the headaches out of choosing all the right components—all you have to do is build the thing!

Components and Software

When we designed the Little Dude, our overriding consideration was always size. Our motto? "Keep it small, stupid." Although we wanted to soup up the Little Dude with serious gaming components and a high-end processor, we were constrained by its size. Small cases tend to store a lot of heat, which is a big problem for machines built for gaming or high-end processing. To solve some of our heat issues, we chose the Shuttle SFF because of how well it handles heat. We were also careful to choose a video card and memory that offered capable cooling solutions.

All of our peripherals had to be small as well, since the Little Dude is designed to be portable. Don't get us wrong, we're not trying to replace the laptop here, but if you're a college student and you go home to visit your family for the weekend, we'd like you to be able to take your PC with you. With the Little Dude, your monitor and speakers are smaller in size, but that doesn't mean they're inferior. We chose only quality parts for this and every system we designed.

Processor

We give you a little bit of a speed boost over the Gamer and recommend an AMD Athlon 64 3400+ processor ($240, www.amd.com) for this Little Dude. Like all AMD processors, this one is a solid performer and a great value for what you get. It comes with a compatible processor cooler, but you won't need that since the Shuttle comes with its own unique cooling system. Codenamed ICE, the Shuttle's cooling system includes a heat sink with radiator pipes and a heat-removing fan. It's really a beauty to look at and keeps your processor nice and cool!

Small Form Factor Bare-Bones System

After much deliberation, we chose the Shuttle XPC SN85G4 ($270, www.shuttle.com). It looks cool and has a reputation in the enthusiast market as one kick-butt SFF. Shuttle was the first in the business to introduce SFF PCs, and we feel that they are slightly ahead of the competition as far as quality, performance, and cooling are concerned.

Like most SFFs, the Shuttle XPC SN85G4 includes a motherboard specifically designed to fit in the case—so there's no need to go shopping for a separate motherboard. This Shuttle's motherboard comes with integrated video and audio chips, your typical large area network (LAN) connection, and an abundance of Universal Serial Bus (USB) ports.

Although we hate to say it, you can use the onboard video if you really need to. We say *need to* because, in our opinion, this should be a last resort and only a temporary solution while you save up for a nice video card.

The onboard sound, however, is another story. We not only recommend that you use it, you pretty much *have* to use it. The accelerated graphics port (AGP) and Peripheral Component Interconnect (PCI) slots are so close together in SFFs that if you use a high-end video card with a big heat sink, you just won't have room for a sound card as well. The good news is that the onboard sound on this motherboard is actually pretty decent. And, remember, you always have to make compromises when you build a smaller PC.

Memory

As with the Gamer, you need more and better memory than you need in other machines. For this configuration, we recommend 1,024 MB (1 GB) of high-performance DDR memory that you can buy from high-end memory producers such as OCZ Technology ($225, www.ocztechnology.com). The OCZ PC3200 DDR memory that we recommend costs about $225 and includes heat spreaders to keep it cool, which is important for gaming rigs and even more important for SFFs being used as gaming rigs. No matter what type of memory you get, make sure it has heat spreaders to assist with cooling.

Video Card

If it's good enough for the Gamer, it's good enough for this Little Dude. Therefore, since we recommended the PowerColor Radeon 9800 Pro ($200, www.power-color.com) for the Gamer, we think the Little Dude should have one too. This card was PowerColor's most expensive video card until the release of ATI's new Radeon X800 graphics processing unit (GPU). It's an awesome card, has great cooling, and powers through even the toughest games.

Hard Drive

Stock your Little Dude with plenty of fast storage by getting a Maxtor 80 GB Serial SATA drive ($75, www.maxtor.com). We thought about going with the Western Digital Raptor drive, which we recommended for the Ultimate Dude, but the heat and noise from that super-fast 10,000 rpm drive just isn't worth the headache.

Optical Drive

Because of heat and space constraints, we suggest adding only one optical drive to this system. The Optorite 16x dual layer DVD burner ($90, www.optorite.com) is a great choice because you can use it to play and burn DVDs and burn music CDs as well. This compact PC is practically designed for high school and college students, and we know they like movies, music, and games.

Sound Card

Unfortunately, you can't fit a sound card into this cramped case. *Fortunately*, the onboard sound isn't that bad. In fact, we hooked up a set of Klipsch ProMedias to it and they sounded okay. There, does that make you feel better?

Modem

No, please no. Actually you don't have any room, so you can't have it without giving up some gaming power. If you don't have access to a cable modem or DSL service, and you still want to build a Little Dude, then you're going to have to make one more compromise.

As we said earlier, with a big, hefty video card, there's no room for a sound card because the one AGP and one PCI slot allotted in this SFF are so close together that an extra card just won't fit. In order to make room for your modem, you're going to have to use a less powerful video card with a smaller heat sink and cooler, such as the PowerColor Radeon 9550 ($80, www.power-color.com) or even the PowerColor Radeon 9250 ($45). This should leave enough room to fit a modem into the only PCI slot in this system. But keep in mind that this machine loses much of its gaming power when you step down the video card.

If you must get a modem, here are some modem manufacturers we've had good luck with: Creative (www.creative.com), CNet (www.cnetusa.com), and Diamond (www.diamondmm.com). A decent value modem will cost you about $15 to $25, or even $10 if you stumble across a really good deal.

Operating System

Games are designed for Windows XP Home Edition ($199, www.microsoft.com), so get it. The major drawback to Windows XP is that it's quite expensive, but you can get it for about half the price ($94) by buying the bundled version with your hardware. This version is for system builders like you and doesn't come with manuals or even technical support. All you get is the CD and the license number that allows you to use the product.

Don't worry about manuals and technical support though, because we take you through a fresh install of Windows XP in Chapter 10. There, we show you step by step how to build one of these cool little machines and install Windows too.

Monitor

The Shuttle SFF case and the Shuttle XP17 17-inch portable LCD ($499, www.shuttle.com) are the coolest parts of this system. This monitor is designed to be rugged because it's made to be mobile. It's constructed of special safety glass and includes a built-in handle and optional bag to make it easy to carry. Sure, the Shuttle XP17 is a little pricey when compared to other 17-inch LCDs, but its special travel features and lightweight portability make it well worth the price. You won't be disappointed. It honestly looks and feels like it will last forever.

Input Devices

If you want to make this little guy really portable, you've gotta go wireless. Logitech sets the bar on quality with the Cordless MX Duo ($75, www.logitech.com). It's more responsive and accurate than other wireless keyboard/mouse combos and it's a great deal at under a hundred bucks.

Speakers

Normally, we only recommend one set of speakers, but if you've got the cash, we suggest getting a set for travel and a set for home. When you're on the road, you're going to have to sacrifice the subwoofer for portability, but the Altec Lansing VS2120 2.0 speakers ($40, www.alteclansing.com) are small, light, and still sound great. When you're not on the road, hook the Little Dude up to a set of Klipsch ProMedia GMX A-2.1 speakers ($140, www.klipsch.com) and make the most of that onboard sound chip.

Chapter 9

Building
A Gamer

//

Are you ready to roll up your sleeves and build a PC from scratch? If you've read the rest of this book, you should be. We already gave you a crash course in PC anatomy with a solid grounding in all the components that make your machine tick or, in this case, kill (we're betting you play a lot of first-person shooters).

We also tried to help you determine just what type of system you need to build. Don't worry if you're not building a Gamer; the components vary from system to system, but the way you snap them all together is pretty much the same. The only big difference comes when you're building a PC using a Small Form Factor (SFF) case, which we explain in the next chapter.

If you've ordered and received all your components (**Table 9.1**), dust 'em off and get ready to put them to work. By the end of this chapter, you'll be ready to build a fully functional PC that wipes the floor with the one you were thinking of buying. Not only that, but you'll have the sense of accomplishment that comes from doing hard things. Not that building a Gamer is all that hard. In fact, we're willing to bet you'll actually enjoy yourself. Ready to have a little fun?

 **Sweeet!**

As you'll see in our pictures, we wear white gloves to prevent the transfer of our body oils to our components. This isn't actually necessary, but we take precautions that aren't always necessary. With white gloves, you accomplish two things: first, you keep your components from collecting your oil, grease, or dirt, and second, you help prevent static, which will definitely ruin your component and your day.

 **Sweeet!**

Read the entire chapter before taking on this project. Doing so will help you see the big picture and make your life easier. Also, our Sweeet tips follow the instructions, so make sure there isn't a tip that goes with a step before you proceed. We don't want you to bang your head on the table saying, "Dang, I wish I knew that five minutes ago."

Table 9.1: **Gamer System Configuration**	
COMPONENT	**RECOMMENDED PRODUCT**
Processor	AMD Athlon 64 3200+ (socket 754)
Motherboard	ASUS K8V (socket 754)
Case and power supply	Antec Sonata
Memory	1,024 MB (1 GB) OCZ PC3200 DDR
Video card	PowerColor Radeon 9800 Pro
Hard drive	Maxtor 80 GB SATA
Optical drive	Lite-On IT 52×32×52×16 DVD-ROM/CD burner combo
Floppy drive	1.44 MB drive
Sound card	Sound Blaster Audigy 2 Value
Modem card	56 Kbps v.90/92
Operating system	Windows XP Home Edition
Monitor	17-inch LCD flat panel
Input devices	Logitech Cordless MX Duo
Speakers	Creative I-Trigue 3400 2.1

Product listings and prices were accurate at the time this book was published. For the most up-to-date products and prices, please visit our Web site at www.dudecomputers.com.

Prep Work

Just like painting the inside of your house, where taping off trim and covering furniture is just as important as the painting itself, prep work is key when it comes to assembling your computer parts. In fact, it's the first thing you do. Prepping the case involves removing all door covers, all slot covers in the back of the case, the drive bays, the hard drive cage, the back-plate, and anything else that is inside your case. The goal is to have a stripped down case that you can build upon.

Remember, you can put everything you remove from the case back in its place later. It's much easier to put everything you've removed back than it is to remove something that's in the way. If you don't remove all the slot covers in the back of the case, for example, you're just hoping that your video card and sound card align with the slot covers you did remove. If you're wrong with your guesstimate, you're going to have to remove the motherboard and try again. Do you have that kind of time to waste? We didn't think so.

How to Prepare the Case

We talked about how important it is to prep your case; now we'll show you. Follow our steps carefully and try not to rush. If you rush, you're likely to miss something, cut up your hands, or bruise your knuckles. Sadly, we speak from experience.

1. On the backside of your case, remove the two thumbscrews. Doing so allows you to remove the side panel so that you can get in there and work.

2. On the side panel, push in the latch, remove the side panel, and set it aside (**Figure 9.1**).

Figure 9.1: Remove the side panel from the case and set it aside.

DUDE, This One Time...

I (Carlito) have been building computers for years and—until recently—never did any prep work to my motherboards or cases. I simply started building with no method to my madness. Often, I would have to remove a drive or motherboard because I forgot to remove a cover or a bay, which would cost me hours of time (and profit).

So when I showed Darrel how to build his first PC, we just started building. After his first build, Darrel went on to build a couple of PCs for his friends and family members. Being the mechanically minded guy that he is, Darrel created his own little system— he stripped down the case and did as much work on the motherboard as he could prior to installing it.

A couple of months after our first build together, we were building a PC for a friend at work and Darrel questioned why I didn't strip the case down or prep the motherboard. My answer was, "Because I just never thought of it." Well, I'm here to tell you, in this case, an old dog can learn new tricks, but more importantly, this prep work is saving me hours these days. So take it from me—do your prep work!

Sweeet!

The hard drive cage is a nice feature available with this case; however, it is not a standard in all cases, especially the cheaper ones. The hard drive cage allows you to install your hard drive easily without having to work inside the case. You can mount the hard drive to the cage, and then just slide the removable cage back into the rack. In this case, the rack can accommodate four hard drives.

Sweeet!

Put all of your screws, covers, and other small parts in one of your component boxes so you don't accidentally lose any of them. Also, leave the CDs that come with the components in their respective boxes so you won't get confused about which CD has the driver for a particular component. You'll have fewer problems during the build if you can stay organized.

3. In the middle of the open side of the case, you'll see the hard drive rack with the hard drive cages installed. Remove all of the cages and set them aside for later use (**Figure 9.2**).

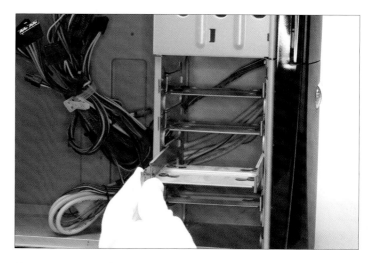

Figure 9.2: Remove the hard drive cages and set them aside.

4. Go to the back of your case and unscrew and remove all of the expansion card slot covers (**Figure 9.3**). You can reinstall the covers for the slots you don't use later.

Figure 9.3: Remove all of the expansion slot covers.

5. Remove all four optical drive bay covers by reaching through the inside of the case and popping them out. They are connected by tabs, so you may need to exert some force (**Figure 9.4**).

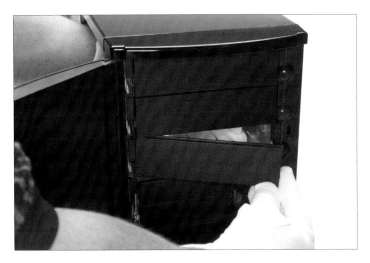

Figure 9.4: Remove the optical drive bay covers by popping them out from the inside of the case.

6. Remove the drive rails from the back of the optical drive bay covers by sliding them out (**Figure 9.5**).

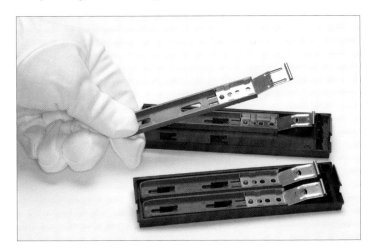

Figure 9.5: Remove the drive rails from the back of the bay covers.

7. Remove the floppy drive cage by pressing in the side tabs and pulling it out (**Figure 9.6**).

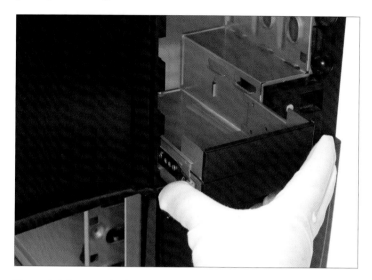

Figure 9.6: Remove the floppy drive bay cover by pressing in on the tabs in the finger cutouts.

Now that you've stripped down your case and removed all the drive bays, covers, and the drive cage, you have extra room to move around inside your case. This makes the rest of the build much easier and may save you from giving your knuckles a bad rap.

How To Prepare the Motherboard

After you've prepped the case, you need to also prep the motherboard, which will save you work and headaches in the long run. In this section, we show you how to inventory the contents of your motherboard box, remove the socket retention screws, install the processor, install the processor cooler, connect all your fans, plug in your memory, and slap on the motherboard back-plate.

You may be asking yourself, "Socket retention screws? What the heck are socket retention screws?" Basically, they hold down your standard heat sink and fan cooler for your processors. We show you how to remove them here because you're going to install an aftermarket processor cooler system that's miles above "standard" and has its own retention system. If you were using a standard processor cooler, such as the one that comes boxed with your processor, then you'd leave the socket retention screws right where they are.

1. Inventory your motherboard contents using the manual, which should list the contents. You just want to make sure that everything on the list is in the box. If you're missing a Serial ATA (SATA) cable or a driver disk, it's better to know now rather than after you've already got the thing built. This is especially true since you'll have to return the motherboard if something critical is missing.

2. After you've determined you have everything you need, lay the motherboard on a flat surface on top of its antistatic bag.

3. The black socket retention frame surrounds the processor socket. Unscrew the socket retention frame screws and remove the frame; this allows you to install the Thermaltake Polo 735 cooler and fan (**Figure 9.7**).

 Sweeet!

Typical items to look for inside the motherboard box are your motherboard, extra USB connectors, serial game port extensions, a floppy drive cable, CD/DVD-ROM cables, IDE hard drive cables, SATA cables, software, and various screws. Always check your manual though; our list is not all inclusive.

 Sweeet!

Always place your motherboard, or any component that you're setting aside or working with, on an antistatic bag to avoid building up an electric charge on the part or getting dirt on it.

Figure 9.7: Unscrew the socket retention frame and remove it.

4. Raise the processor socket lever, which serves as a lock for the processor. When the lever is in the down (locked) position, it grabs the pins on the bottom of the processor and assures electrical contact with the motherboard (**Figure 9.8**).

Figure 9.8: Raise the processor socket lever to unlock the socket.

5. Insert the processor by aligning the triangle on the processor with the triangle on the socket—the triangle has three pins across the angle and the rest have only two (**Figure 9.9**).

Figure 9.9: Insert the processor in the socket making sure to align the triangle on the processor with the triangle on the socket.

6. Push down the socket lever until you hear it click into place.

7. Next, install the processor heat sink and fan assembly. It consists of two parts: the heat sink, which looks like a radiator, and the fan, which sits on top of the heat sink. If you blew through step 3 and did *not* remove the socket retention frame, do so at this time. The Thermaltake Polo 735 cooler (the whole assembly) has different instructions for different motherboards. For this board, use the K8 installation instructions. You must separate the fan from the heat sink, install the I-bar, and then reassemble (**Figure 9.10**).

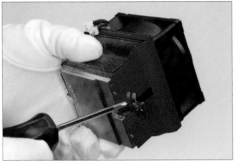

Figure 9.10: Install the heat sink I-bar so the heat sink is ready to install on the processor.

 **Sweeet!**

We highly recommend that you use a thermal compound to help cool your processor. To apply it, place a dab the size of a dime on top of the processor and spread it thinly and evenly using a plastic card. Make sure the layer is smooth and thin—more is not better in this case. Thermal compound is often provided with your fan. If you bought a retail fan, you'll find a piece of thermal tape on the bottom of the cooler.

8. Spread a thin layer of thermal compound, such as Arctic Silver, on top of your processor. The thermal compound allows more heat to transfer from the processor to your cooler (**Figure 9.11**).

Figure 9.11: Spread a thin layer of thermal compound on the processor.

Sweeet!

Installation of these aftermarket coolers varies from product to product and manufacturer to manufacturer, so you'll need to refer to the manual that comes with the cooler you are installing. For this build, we're installing a Thermaltake Polo 735. We recommend using the instructions that come with this cooler along with our instructions.

Sweeet!

Standard coolers usually don't come with fan controllers. High-end coolers include fan controllers so that you can customize your cooler's fan speed and noise. The faster your fan, the louder your computer. We explain how to install the controller after we tell you how to secure the motherboard in the case.

9. After you've applied the thermal compound, place the heat sink and fan cooler on top of the processor and screw them into place (**Figure 9.12**).

Figure 9.12: Place the heat sink and fan assembly on top of the processor and screw them down.

10. Make the wire connection to the motherboard by plugging in the plug with the single yellow wire to the connector on the motherboard labeled "CPU Fan;" this connector is located just above the processor socket (**Figure 9.13**).

Figure 9.13: Connect the single yellow wire to the motherboard in the socket labeled "CPU Fan."

11. Install your memory by pulling out the DIMM slot tabs and pushing your memory sticks into DIMM slots 1 and 3 until you hear a click. Make sure your memory is securely installed by checking that the slot tabs are firmly pressed in (**Figure 9.14**).

Figure 9.14: Pull out on the tabs at the end of the DIMM slots to unlock the DIMMs. Install the memory into the DIMMs one at a time. Make sure you align the notches in the memory and the DIMMs.

12. Remove the back-plate from the back of the case (**Figure 9.15**). To do so, simply push on the back-plate from outside the case; it should pop right out.

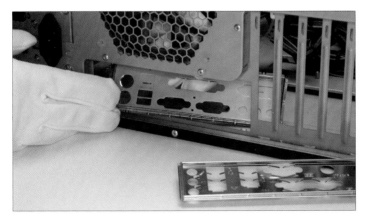

Figure 9.15: Remove the back-plate from the case by pushing it into the case from the outside.

 **Sweeet!**

Make sure that your memory is aligned with the DIMM slot notch prior to applying any real pressure to it. The memory only goes in one way. Look at it closely; you can see that it has a long row of contacts on one side of a notch and a row that is shorter on the other side. Now look at the DIMM slot; it is arranged the same way. If you check this first and the white tabs/locks are in the open position, which is away from the DIMM, then you can't go wrong. It takes some force to get your memory inserted, but if you don't have it properly aligned, you may be in trouble. You can break the memory, or even worse, damage the DIMM slot by trying to force the memory in the wrong way. Push it in evenly and firmly until the memory clicks into place; the click is the sound of the locks snapping closed.

Sweeet!

The back-plate is a cover that allows all your motherboard connectors, such as USB, FireWire, mouse, and keyboard connectors to be accessible for use. To date, we haven't been able to use the one that comes with the case. This is because each motherboard is so different and unique that each usually requires a custom back-plate for its particular connections. All motherboards come with a custom back-plate, which you'll install in the next step.

13. Install the custom motherboard back-plate. It pops into place from inside the case; in other words, you don't need any screws. Think about how the motherboard will lie in the case; this will keep you from installing it upside down (**Figure 9.16**).

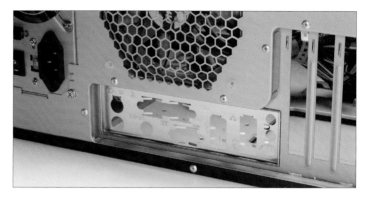

Figure 9.16: Install the custom back-plate supplied with the motherboard.

If you've followed our directions, you should be done prepping the motherboard, which means you've installed the processor, cooler, and memory. As you can tell by now, prepping the motherboard is a lot of work, but trust us, it's much easier to do this outside of the case than to work in a more cramped environment. Next, you'll secure that motherboard to your case.

Installing Components

This part of the build is really fairly easy if you follow along closely. The systematic approach we give you, however, is not written down anywhere else that we know of—so be sure to pay attention. Although we developed the following techniques from numerous trials and errors, we want you to get it right the first time!

How to Install the Motherboard

In the following steps, you'll place and secure the motherboard inside your case. This isn't terribly difficult, just be sure you don't bang the board into any sharp edges or metal pieces on your way in.

1. Install the motherboard screw anchors that were included with the accessories that came with your motherboard.

2. Gently place your motherboard in the case (aligned with the screw anchors) and screw the motherboard into place by placing the screws through the motherboard and into the screw anchors (**Figure 9.17**). All the screws and anchors are included with your motherboard.

Figure 9.17: Install the motherboard in the case and secure it to the anchors with screws.

3. Now, you need to plug in the front panel connectors. This can be a pain, but you need to make sure you do it right. The wires from the front panel are for the audio tones (trouble tones), hard drive light, power light, power switch, and reset switch. The connectors are labeled accordingly. Plug them in according to the diagram for the front panel connectors that's found in your motherboard manual (**Figure 9.18**).

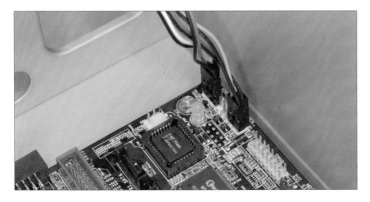

Figure 9.18: Make all the front panel connections to the motherboard.

 **Sweeet!**

These screw anchors are threaded on one side and open on the other. They screw into case holes and allow you to place the motherboard on top of the anchors. You can then secure the motherboard in place by putting screws through the motherboard holes and into the anchors themselves. Make sure the holes in your motherboard line up with the holes you screw your anchors into. A good technique is to lay your motherboard in your case and mark off the holes that line up with a permanent marker. Then remove the motherboard and screw your anchors in.

 **Sweeet!**

Triangles on front panel connectors designate where pin 1 is. Look closely at the motherboard and its manual and you'll see a small number 1 at one end of the pins on the board. The triangle on the connector should be oriented toward the number 1 side of the pins. Be patient and get your entire front panel connected right the first time. If you rush, chances are you'll be in there later trying to figure out why your front panel lights don't work or why your power light won't come on.

4. On your cooler fan, find the Fan Only power plug and connect it to one of the empty 4-pin power source cables from your power supply (**Figure 9.19**).

Figure 9.19: Connect the fan power to one of the 4-pin power cables from the power supply.

5. Grab the 24-pin power source from your power supply cables and plug this into your motherboard's 24-pin power connector—it's located right next to the processor socket. Take the 4-pin square power plug and connect this into your motherboard as well; this connection is right next to the 24-pin connector (**Figure 9.20**).

Figure 9.20: Connect the 24-pin and square 4-pin power cables to the motherboard.

How to Install the Video Card

Installing the video card is pretty simple as long as you make sure you find the accelerated graphics port (AGP) slot. There are Peripheral Component Interconnect (PCI) video cards available, but that's old technology. We haven't used PCI video cards in years. PCI Xpress video cards are also available, but that technology is too new and needs to mature before we jump onboard. AGP cards are just right.

1. Locate the AGP slot—it's the top slot and the darker of the six slots for the cards. This slot has a white clip labeled "AGP" that secures your video card in place (**Figure 9.21**).

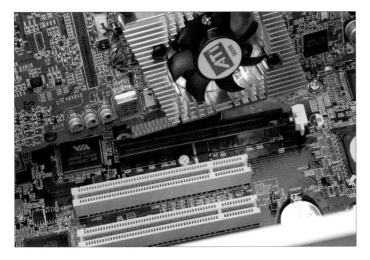

Figure 9.21: Install the video card in the AGP slot.

2. Align the video card with the AGP slot and push it into place until you hear it click.

3. Check to make sure the clip is secured to the AGP card notch by pushing up on the clip. It will be obvious if the clip is securely situated in the notch.

Sweeet!

Make sure you pull back the white clip at the end of the slot before you try to install the video card; if you don't, it won't go in.

4. Plug one of your empty power supply sources into your video card. Most video cards do not require additional power, but this high-end card needs a little extra juice (**Figure 9.22**).

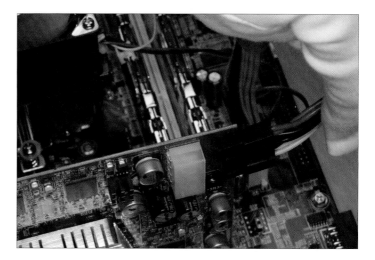

Figure 9.22: Plug in power to the video card.

5. Screw the card into place using one of the screws from the expansion slot covers—remember, we had you remove all of them when you were prepping the case. If you followed the directions, you will find those screws in the box where we told you to put all of your spare parts. You must screw down all of your AGP and PCI cards to make them more secure. The screws go through the top of the metal part of the card and into the holes in the slot openings. You'll tighten the screws to the specifications in the next step.

6. This is where we get technical. Here are the torque specifications for *all* the screws you install: snug them up, when the screw stops turning, stop twisting.

How to Install the Sound Card

It's time to install one of the Gamer's best upgrades. You could, of course, save money by using the onboard audio that comes included on the motherboard, but your Gamer would suffer for it. This Sound Blaster card adds realism to your gaming experience, keeps your system from slowing down, and produces kick-butt audio.

1. Locate the PCI slots on your motherboard; they are located directly underneath the AGP slot and are labeled "PCI."

2. Plug your sound card into one of the PCI slots—it doesn't matter which one because all PCI slots serve the same function (**Figure 9.23**). We normally skip a slot and use the second PCI slot to allow more space for airflow between the AGP card and the sound card.

Figure 9.23: Install the sound card in one of the empty PCI slots.

3. Just like you did with the video card, screw the sound card into place at the slot opening.

How to Install the Fan Controller

You don't have to install the fan controller, but it's nice to be able to regulate your processor fan speed. That way, if the fan is too noisy, you can turn it down or, if you suspect your processor is getting hot, you can turn it up. If you decide not to use the controller, the fan runs at a default speed that may or may not be suitable for you. It's much better to have control over a fan that is this powerful and noisy, which is why we advise you to install the controller.

There are two controllers provided in the Thermaltake Polo 735 package: one that you can install in the front of the case in an empty floppy drive bay, and one that you can install in an empty slot at the back of your case. We prefer the empty slot in the back because it is

Sweeet!

The fan controller that you installed in the back of your case has only one set of wires coming from it. The plug at the end of those wires only connects to its appropriate partner on the fan, making this connection a pretty easy one to make.

out of the way and inaccessible by our little munchkins. You install them both the same way as far as the connections are concerned— the only difference is how you mount it.

If you read the instructions provided with the fan, you'll see that there are three ways to hook it up. Here's how we advise you to hook up the fan controller to an empty slot in the back of the case.

1. Secure the Thermaltake Polo 735 fan controller to the last empty slot at the back of your case. This controller fits right into an empty slot that used to be occupied by a slot cover (**Figure 9.24**).

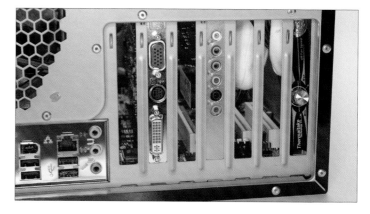

Figure 9.24: Install the Polo fan controller in one of the empty slot cover spaces.

2. Connect the fan controller to the Thermaltake Polo 735 (**Figure 9.25**).

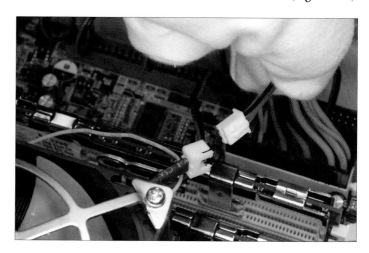

Figure 9.25: Connect the fan controller to the fan.

How to Install the Hard Drive

Installing the hard drive is fairly simple. The one thing you want to remember though is to set your jumpers prior to installing your drive. If you forget, you'll have to uninstall the drive and redo this section all over again.

Sweeet!

If you're setting up a system with more than one hard drive (which we don't like to do or recommend), then you'll need to set one hard drive to master and the other to slave. When you're only setting up one drive, you must set it to master or it will not work.

1. In back of the hard drive, set your jumper to master (MA). You do this by ensuring that the plastic jumper covers the pins that follow the sequence for MA. Your other option is slave (SL), but that only comes into play if you're installing more than one drive (**Figure 9.26**).

Figure 9.26: Set the hard drive jumper to master (MA).

2. Fasten the hard drive to the cage using the four screws that were provided with your case (**Figure 9.27**).

Figure 9.27: Attach the hard drive to the mount using the four screws provided with your case.

Sweeet!

Most of the new power supplies have a SATA power cable coming directly from them. The ones that don't almost always come with an adapter cable. The adapter goes from a regular 4-pin power connecter to a SATA power connector. When you're using a SATA hard drive, you must use the SATA power connector.

Sweeet!

Make sure you route all your SATA and hard drive cables neatly through the bottom of the hard drive rack prior to plugging them into the hard drive. This helps your build stay neat and orderly and prevents these items from restricting airflow.

3. At the back of the hard drive, plug in the SATA cable and the power cable. The SATA cable is red and thin and looks like no other cable. This cable also has a connector with an "L" shape to make orientation easier. The power cable will have a STAT type connector also (**Figure 9.28**).

Figure 9.28: Connect a SATA cable to the back of the hard drive.

4. Slide the hard drive in the hard drive rack; any slot is OK, but we normally use the first or second slot. Carefully route the SATA and power cables smoothly through the hard drive rack as you insert the drive. The drive should click into place and lock on the tabs (**Figure 9.29**).

Figure 9.29: Slide the hard drive back into the rack until it snaps in place.

5. Place the remaining empty hard drive cages back into the hard drive rack for safe keeping.

6. Take the SATA cable that you just plugged into your hard drive and routed through the hard drive rack and plug it into the SATA terminal labeled "SATA 1" on your motherboard. Take a look at **Figure 9.30**; it shows a pretty clear shot of the SATA terminal with the cable plugged in. On the motherboard, the terminals are located between the processor and the video card.

Figure 9.30: Connect the SATA cable to the motherboard and plug the cable to the SATA connection labeled "SATA 1."

How to Install the Optical Drives

It's finally time to install the drives that let you play all your software, movies, and games. This rig is a two optical drive system with one drive being a DVD-ROM and the other a CD burner. This is a pretty standard setup that we've been building with for years.

1. On the back of the DVD-ROM drive, set the jumper to master as you did with your hard drive (**Figure 9.31**). One of the drives has to be master and one has to be slave because they are both connected to the same cable. The master drive is the one that your PC looks for when you're installing the operating system, so make sure you put your Windows CD into this drive when it's time to load up Windows.

Figure 9.31: Set the jumper on the back of the DVD-ROM to master (MA).

Sweeet!

You don't have to put all the empty hard drive cages back into place in order for your PC to work, it just makes it easier to find them if you want to add an extra drive later.

Sweeet!

Just to keep things standard, we install the DVD-ROM on top of the CD or DVD burner and set the DVD-ROM to master and the burner to slave. If you set things up this way every time, you always know which drive is your master drive. It is important that you know this because when you go to load Windows, your computer only looks for the Windows disk in the master drive.

Sweeet!

About the screws—you get some with the drive in a retail package, but the motherboard and case manufacturers normally give you some too. Just find the ones that fit; there are only about four types of screws used in a computer build and it's not difficult to eliminate the ones that do not fit or work.

2. On the back of the CD burner drive, set the jumper to slave.

3. Install the rails to both of the drives by screwing one rail to each side of the drives. These are the rails that you removed from the back of those plastic optical drive bay covers when you were prepping the case (**Figure 9.32**).

Figure 9.32: Install the rails to the sides of the DVD-ROM and CD burner with screws that fit.

4. Now you need the floppy drive cage you removed way back when you prepped the case. This cage has two blanking plates installed. Remove the lower one; this is where the floppy drive is going to live.

5. Slide the floppy drive into the floppy drive cage. Install two screws in each side of the cage (**Figure 9.33**).

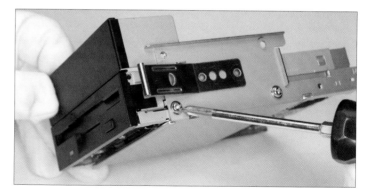

Figure 9.33: Install the floppy drive in the cage and secure it with screws that fit.

6. Slide the floppy drive cage back into the case (**Figure 9.34**).

Figure 9.34: Install the floppy drive in the case.

7. In the upper bay slot on the front of the machine, slide in your DVD-ROM drive until you hear it click (**Figure 9.35**).

Figure 9.35: Install the DVD-ROM in the case.

8. In the third bay slot from the top on the front of your machine, slide in the CD-ROM drive until you hear it click.

9. Plug the twisted end of the floppy drive cable into the back of the floppy drive. This cable is included with your motherboard and is the only cable we have found that can be put in the wrong way. Just make sure that the white stripe faces toward the inside of the case and the word "ASUS" on the cable is facing up. Look at **Figure 9.36**; it will help you make sense of this.

Figure 9.36: Plug in the floppy cable to the floppy drive.

10. Plug the opposite end of the floppy drive cable into the motherboard slot labeled "floppy" making sure that the striped side of the ribbon cable is facing the front of the case. This connection is keyed with a missing pin in the receptacle and a blank in the plug (**Figure 9.37**).

Figure 9.37: Plug the floppy cable into the motherboard to the socket labeled "Floppy."

11. Connect a free power connector from your power supply to the back of your floppy drive. The connector used by the floppy is smaller than the big 4-pin connectors used on the other devices. This power plug connects to the back of the floppy drive right next to the data cable you installed in step 9; take a look at Figure 9.36 again and you will see the connections.

12. Grab the IDE cable supplied with your motherboard. This cable is designed to hook up two optical drives to one IDE connector on the motherboard. Start at your DVD-ROM and plug in the end that has the shortest amount of wire between the plugs. All of these connections are keyed, so take a look at the plugs and the sockets they go to before you try to cram them together. Connect the next plug to the CD drive and then connect the end of the cable to the IDE socket labeled "Pri_ IDE" on the motherboard (**Figures 9.38** and **9.39**).

Figure 9.38: Connect the IDE cable to the optical drives.

Figure 9.39: Connect the IDE cable to the socket labeled "IDE 1."

Congratulations! The building part is over. The inside of your finished PC should look similar to **Figure 9.40**. The outside of your Gamer should look similar to **Figure 9.41**.

Figure 9.40: The inside of your new computer should look like this picture.

Figure 9.41: Take a look at the outside of your sweeet, new PC.

Did you think it would ever come to an end? Just kidding—we bet you had a blast and learned a bunch in the process. Now you have a working PC that needs an operating system and some software to get you in the action. In the next section, we show you how to install Windows and some very useful software.

Setting Up the BIOS

BIOS, which stands for Basic Input/Output System, is the onboard programming that allows your motherboard and components to communicate at the most basic levels. It allows you to configure how everything will work. You'll use the BIOS to configure your controllers and drives and set the date and time for your PC. You'll only use the BIOS to configure devices until you install your operating system, so don't plan on adopting it as your new word processor or anything. It's not that kind of software.

Before setting up your BIOS, read your motherboard manual. The manual explains, in great detail, what settings are available to you and how you can configure all your devices. We always read manuals; you should get into the same habit to avoid problems later. Right now though, we're going to walk you through our short BIOS setup.

How to Set Up Your BIOS

The first thing you need to do when you set up the BIOS is choose *default* or *optimized* settings. These settings provide you with a foundation from which to start your BIOS customization. After you have chosen these, you can customize them to your specific needs.

In the following steps, we first show you exactly how to choose these settings and then how to customize them. In doing so, we hope to explain a little bit of our reasoning. In other words, it wouldn't be entirely fair to you if we simply just told you "how;" we want to fill in some of the "what" and the "why" as well. Don't worry if this is a little confusing, we show you how to set this stuff up step by step. Let's get into it.

1. Power on your Gamer and immediately press the Delete key repeatedly to enter the BIOS Setup Utility. It doesn't matter how many times you press the Delete key, just keep pressing it until you enter the BIOS Setup Utility.

2. In the BIOS Setup Utility, use your arrow keys to highlight the Exit menu at the top of the screen; this will bring up the Exit options. The next step explains how to load setup defaults.

Sweeet!

You can always turn off your system by pressing the power button for about five seconds, and then you can reenter the BIOS by pressing the Delete key as the computer powers up. This is a good thing to know for the future—you may need it. When you're navigating the BIOS menu, you use the arrow keys, the Tab key, or the Scroll key to move the highlighted cursor up, down, left, and right. The + (plus) and − (minus) keys allow you to select some settings. To select a menu item, use the Enter key, and to back out of a menu, use the Esc key. These are basic functions and are the same for all of the BIOS systems we have experienced.

3. Use your arrow keys to scroll down to Load Setup Defaults. Press the Enter key to load these (**Figure 9.42**). By pressing Enter, you load the starting point/foundation we spoke of earlier, meaning that you are loading the basic settings that make the computer function. Keep in mind that if you ever think you may have messed up a setting, you can always go back, reload the defaults, and start over. Next, we'll show you how to customize these settings for your system.

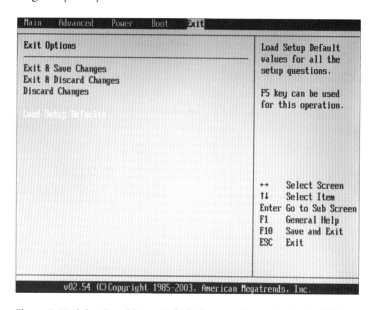

Figure 9.42: Select "Load Setup Defaults" as a starting point for the BIOS.

4. Use your arrow keys to scroll to the Boot menu and then press Enter (**Figure 9.43**).

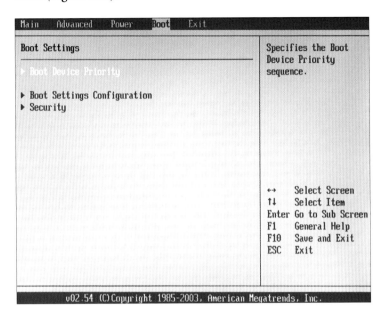

Figure 9.43: Select the Boot menu.

5. Set boot device priority by highlighting the primary drive selection and toggling through with the + or – keys. Do the same for the secondary and tertiary devices.

We like booting the floppy first, the DVD-ROM or CD-ROM second, and the hard drive third. This way, the computer looks for a recovery disk in the floppy drive first (some antivirus programs have floppy emergency recovery disks), a recovery or operating system CD from the optical drive second, and then lastly, if it doesn't find any of these (which is usually the case), it looks for your hard drive and loads up your computer (**Figure 9.44**).

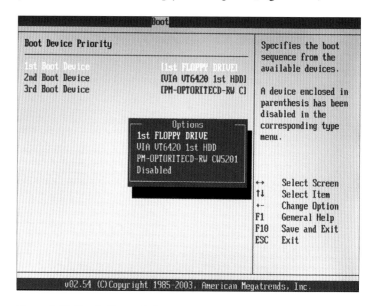

Figure 9.44: Set the Boot priority.

6. Now, using the arrow keys, highlight the Advanced menu, arrow down to Chipset, and press Enter. Select AGP Bridge Configuration and press Enter.

7. In the Chipset submenu, arrow down to Primary Graphics
    Adapter and, using the + or – keys, toggle until AGP is displayed
    (**Figure 9.45**). In this manner, you set up your video card as the
    primary video output.

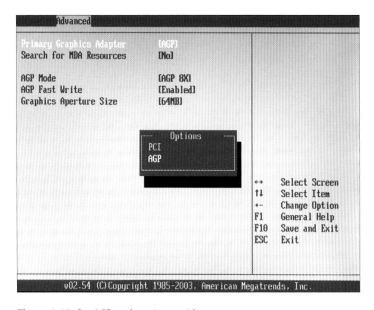

Figure 9.45: Set AGP as the primary video output.

8. Press Escape twice to go back to the Main BIOS Setup Utility
    window. Select Onboard Devices Configuration, and press Enter.
    Select Disable for the Onboard AC'97 Audio. By doing this, you're
    disabling your onboard (integrated) audio and setting your sound
    card as the primary audio output.

 **Sweeet!**

Before you exit the BIOS, you always
have a chance to cancel your settings.
The options are Exit and Save Changes,
Exit and Discard Changes, Discard
Changes, or Load Setup Defaults, so if
you think you goofed up, you can exit
without saving and start over.

9. Press Escape, which returns you to the Advanced menu. Using your arrow keys select Main in the top navigation bar. Within the Main menu, arrow down and set your time (**Figure 9.46**).

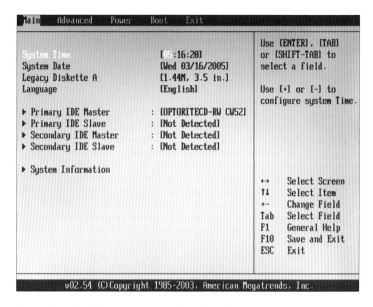

Figure 9.46: Set the date and time from the Main menu.

10. While you're in the Main menu, you should also set the date. To do so, use your arrow keys to highlight the date and enter today's date.

11. Scroll with the right arrow key to the Exit menu. In this menu, select Exit and Save Changes and click OK (**Figure 9.47**).

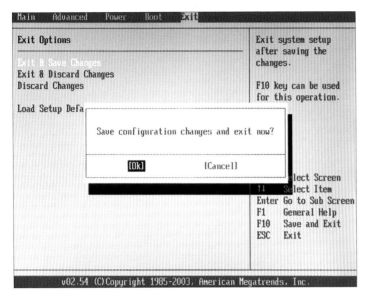

Figure 9.47: Choose "Exit and Save Changes" from the Exit menu.

See, that wasn't so bad. You've just completed the basic setup that your components require to communicate with each other and function optimally. Now, it's time to install your actual operating system (OS).

 **Sweeet!**

These are *our* preferred settings. Others may agree or disagree with these, but we like to strike a balance between performance and stability. We feel that the settings we provide give you a stable system and that with these settings, your components will run as fast as possible without being the least bit shaky. After all, there's no sense in setting up a fast machine that is unstable or unusable at times.

Installing Windows XP Home Edition

Now that you've put this sweet machine together and set up your BIOS, it's time to load up Windows. Windows XP Home Edition is what makes everything come together; it's what allows your software to talk with your components and make them work. Even if you don't have any other software installed, Windows XP gives you a basic bundle that allows you to configure an Internet and/or email account, write plain text in Notepad, burn CDs, chat via Windows Messenger, and play music CDs. It even includes a couple of basic games, such as Classic Solitaire and FreeCell.

Installing Windows can be confusing if you don't know what you're doing. It's not difficult, but if you don't know much about what settings you prefer, your installation may take longer or you may have to reconfigure some items after the installation. Don't worry though, we're about to show you the best way to configure your operating system so that you can get the most out of your new machine.

Having Problems With Your Windows Install?

If the Windows XP installer won't recognize your hard drive, you'll probably have to install third-party SATA drivers, which should be found on the CD or companion floppy disk that came with your motherboard. If your motherboard manufacturer didn't provide a floppy disk with SATA drivers, then you'll have to extract the drivers from the motherboard's CD and save them to a floppy. For the Gamer, we had to extract the VIA 6420 SATA drivers from the CD. If you don't already have a computer, get on a friend's computer, use your computer at work, or go to your local library and follow these steps.

1. Install the CD that came with your motherboard.

2. Double-click "My Computer."

3. Right-click on the CD drive and select "Explore."

4. Double-click the "Drivers" folder.

5. Double-click the "VIA RAID" folder.

6. Double-click the "Driver Disk" folder.

7. Insert a blank floppy disk into the floppy drive.

8. Double-click the "Make Disk" icon.

You've just created a floppy disk with your drivers stored on it. During the Windows XP install, you'll need to take a few extra steps to install them. On initial setup, you'll be prompted to "Press F6 to install 3rd party SCSI driver." Press F6. Next, Windows Setup will prompt you to specify the device for which you have a disk. Press "S." Follow the prompts to insert the floppy disk and press "Enter." The next screen asks you to select the SATA driver for your operating system. Select "VIA Serial ATA RAID Controller (Windows XP)." After the drivers are copied to your setup files by the installer, follow the prompt and press "Enter" to continue the installation. Windows will continue installing and the installer will take you to the Welcome Setup screen as seen in Figure 9.48.

How to Install Windows XP

1. Insert the Windows XP Installation CD into your drive.

2. Restart your computer by pressing the reset switch.

3. When your computer restarts, it takes you to the Windows XP Home Edition Setup page.

4. In the Windows XP Home Edition Setup menu, press Enter to select the option "To Setup Windows XP now" (**Figure 9.48**).

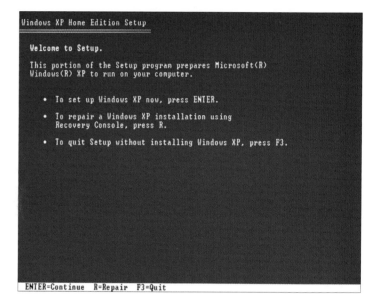

Figure 9.48: Select "To Setup Windows XP now Press ENTER" and press the Enter key.

5. Read the Windows XP Licensing Agreement and press the F8 key to continue.

6. Use your up and down arrow keys to select "To set up Windows XP on the selected item, press ENTER" and then press the Enter key (**Figure 9.49**). If this is a brand new hard drive (as is the case for most of you), or if you only have one hard drive installed (which we highly recommend), then you only see one item to select labeled, "Unpartitioned Space." In this case, just press the Enter key.

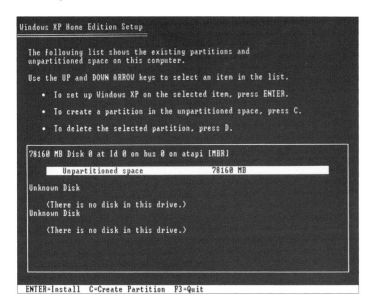

Figure 9.49: Select "To set up Windows XP on the selected item, press ENTER" and press the Enter key.

7. Select "Format the partition using the NTFS file system" and press the Enter key (**Figure 9.50**). Don't choose the Quick option unless you've formatted your hard drive once before. The first time you format a drive it should be a regular format.

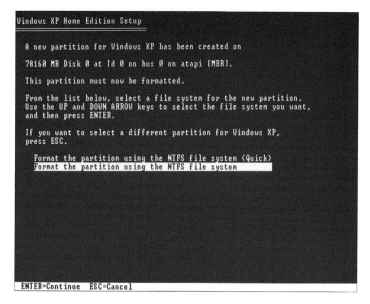

Figure 9.50: Select "Format the partition using the NTFS file system" and press the Enter key.

8. After your PC is done formatting your hard drive and copying setup files, let it reboot automatically. You could press Enter to restart, but we prefer to wait, just in case Windows is doing something behind the scenes. After restart, Windows continues with setup.

9. As Windows loads, it asks you to make some choices. When the Regional and Language Options window appears, click Next, unless you speak Swahili or something other than English and want to customize the language.

10. In the Personalize Your Software window, type in your name and click Next.

11. In the Your Product Key window, enter your product key—it's that really cool-looking and colorful sticker that comes on the outside of your Windows disk and has about 200 characters in the code. After you enter this code, which actually has only 25 characters, go ahead and click Next (**Figure 9.51**). Put that sticker on your computer because it's the only evidence you have that you bought Windows. That code cost you in the neighborhood of $100, so don't lose it.

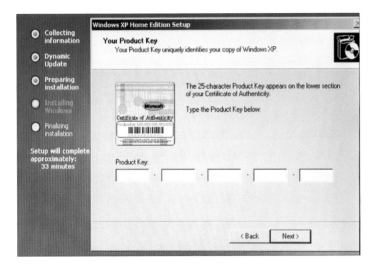

Figure 9.51: Enter your Windows product key.

12. In the What's Your Computer's Name? window, type in a name for your computer. It can be anything you want—we usually go with Greek Gods. Click Next when you've decided.

13. In the Date and Time Settings window, choose your date, time, and time zone from their respective menus and click Next.

14. In the Network Settings window, click the button next to Typical Settings to select it and click Next.

15. Windows reboots automatically one final time before installation is complete, and upon startup, it takes you to a Welcome screen. Click Next to continue.

16. In the Help Protect Your PC window, select whether or not you would like to activate automatic updates and then click Next. We suggest you select the automatic updates to stay up-to-date.

17. In the Registration window, you're asked to register your copy of Windows. Chances are good that you don't have an Internet connection yet, so click Skip to skip registration now and register later over the Internet or phone. Microsoft allows you 30 days to register before it sends out the goons to bust your kneecaps; just make sure you register within the allotted time or your machine will stop working and you'll have to start all over again with your Windows installation. To register, all you need is your product key; there isn't a separate registration number.

18. In the Who Will Use This Computer? window, type in the names of all the people who will use the computer and click Next.

That's it for setting up Windows. Now, let's load some drivers.

Installing Drivers and Software

After you've performed the initial setup, Windows should load a clean, empty desktop onto your monitor (**Figure 9.52**). This clean desktop has Windows installed, but you still need to load *drivers*, which basically allow Windows to recognize and communicate with your components. Without drivers, your computer does not run optimally.

Figure 9.52: This is a clean desktop.

In this section, you'll also learn to install some software that comes bundled with your sound card, video card, and optical drives. Why do you need to do all this? To make your computer more powerful and functional.

 **Sweeet!**

Bundled software is a great way to make your computer more productive without having to spend money on software solutions. We love Media Player, which is bundled with the Sound Blaster cards, and the Nero burning software that's bundled with many CD/DVD burners. We also like the DVD players that are bundled with video cards and the utility tools that are bundled with motherboards. It's all great software, and like we said, it improves your computing experience and saves you money.

How to Install Motherboard Drivers

Without motherboard drivers, your motherboard will not function correctly. These drivers allow the motherboard to communicate with all the external cards, processors, memory, and drives attached to it.

1. Insert the CD-ROM that came with your motherboard.

2. In the Drivers menu that appears, click VIA 4 in 1 drivers option and install all the drivers (**Figure 9.53**).

Figure 9.53: Check VIA 4 in 1 drivers to install all of your motherboard drivers.

3. Restart Windows XP when you are directed to do so.

How to Install Video Card Drivers

Your computer would probably still work without video card drivers, but to get the most out of your video card, you should install its drivers. Windows XP has built-in drivers that allow the user's video to function, but the end result is not the best.

1. Insert the CD-ROM that came with your video card. The CD should automatically load and take you to the setup screen.

2. In the setup screen, choose "Display Adapter Driver Setup" to install all necessary drivers and software on your PC (**Figure 9.54**).

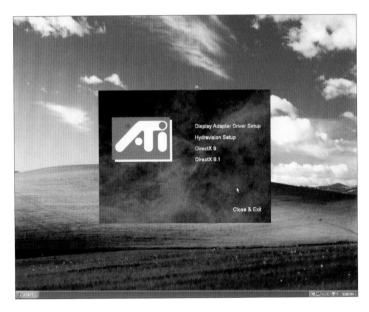

Figure 9.54: Install the ATI video drivers.

3. After the drivers and software are installed, you're prompted to restart your computer. Go ahead and check "Yes" when directed. Your drivers and/or software won't work properly until you restart your computer.

How to Install Sound Card Drivers

As we explained with the video card, Windows XP has basic drivers built in that allow your sound card to function as well. In order to get the best sound, however, you need to install the supplied sound card drivers.

1. Insert the CD-ROM that came with your Sound Blaster Audigy 2 sound card.

2. In the setup menu that appears, choose "Americas" for your region.

3. When the Sound Blaster Audigy 2 window appears, click "Next" and follow the auto install directions (**Figure 9.55**).

Figure 9.55: Install the Audigy 2 drivers for your sound card.

4. When prompted to restart your computer, select "Yes."

Chapter 10

Building
A Little Dude

We used to be big believers in towers with all the fixin's, but if you're
not into extreme gaming or multimedia work, the Little Dude is a great
choice and it's really easy to build. The only reason we didn't recommend
the Little Dude for the Internet Surfer or the Home Office PC is because it
costs a little more. That said, if you have some extra cash and don't need
a powerhouse of a machine, you can build an Internet Surfer or Home
Office PC in a Small Form Factor (SFF) box for only about $150 extra.

The Gamer and Multimedia PCs, however, really require more drives,
more power, much better cooling, and add-on sound cards, so you
need the bigger cases for these. SFF PCs have a Peripheral Component
Interconnect (PCI) slot where technically, you could plug in a sound
card, but the heat sink and fans on today's high-powered video cards
prevent this from being feasible because the cards tend to touch and
block airflow. We hope Shuttle and other SFF companies will correct this
and we'll make such recommendations to them. In the meantime, you
have to make some compromises. The onboard sound in this Little Dude
is acceptable, but it is nowhere near the quality of the recommended
sound cards in our other builds.

Sweeet!

As you'll notice in *Table 10.1*, there is no floppy drive required for this build. Instead, we chose a Shuttle SFF with a built-in card reader, which can read memory cards used by digital cameras, mp3 players, and personal digital assistants (PDAs). If you still transfer files to and from work on a floppy, we recommend you switch to a USB flash drive or save your data to a PDA.

That said, the beauty of building your own PC is that your component choices are endless. This Little Dude is an affordable powerhouse only because we designed and built it ourselves. This level of performance at this price point is only possible by building the beast with your own two hands.

Before you get started with the build, inventory your parts to make sure you have everything you need to successfully complete it (**Table 10.1**)—we don't want you to have to stop midway because you forgot to order your DVD burner. Don't throw out any of your manuals, either. Although we tell you everything you need to know to build your computer from the ground up, your manuals offer a ton of valuable information and can answer many of your questions should you get lost along the way.

Table 10.1: **Little Dude System Configuration**	
COMPONENT	RECOMMENDED PRODUCT
Processor	AMD Athlon 64 3400+ (socket 754)
Small Form Factor	Shuttle XPC SN85G4 (socket 754)
Memory	1 GB OCZ PC3200 DDR
Video card	PowerColor Radeon 9800 Pro
Hard drive	Maxtor 80 GB SATA
Optical drive	Optorite 16x dual-layer DVD burner
Sound card	Integrated
Operating system	Windows XP Home Edition
Monitor	Shuttle XP17 17-inch portable LCD
Input devices	Logitech Cordless MX Duo
Speakers	Altec Lansing VS2120

Product listings and prices were accurate at the time this book was published. For the most up-to-date products and prices, please see our Web site at www.dudecomputers.com.

Prep Work

Before you can start installing components, you'll need to do a little prep work. The first thing you need to do is remove the case cover and the drive rack. OK. Let's get started!

How to Remove the Case Cover

This case is simplicity at its best. We have yet to find any easier computer to build. The case design allows you to remove the cover in two easy steps and grants you full and fast access to the internals.

1. Flip the case over and unscrew and remove the three thumb-screws that secure the case cover to the rest of the case. Set these thumbscrews in a safe place and don't lose them; you'll need them again when you finish building this computer (**Figure 10.1**).

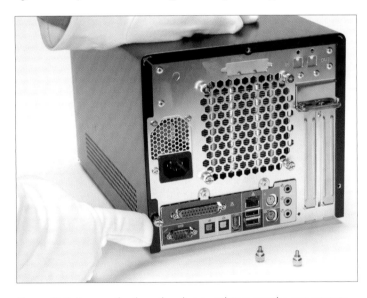

Figure 10.1: Remove the three thumbscrews that secure the case cover to the case and put them in a safe place.

2. Return the case to its upright position and slide the cover back and up to remove it (**Figure 10.2**).

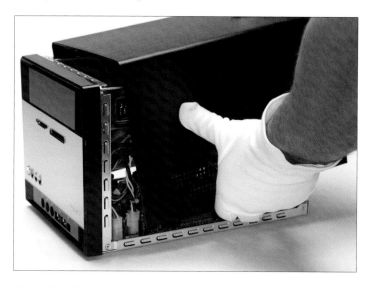

Figure 10.2: Slide the case cover first slightly back, then up, to remove it.

How to Remove the Drive Rack

The drive rack, which is at the front of the machine, holds your hard drive and optical drive. You can remove the drive rack from the case, which is convenient because doing so allows you to install your drives without having to work in the cramped environment of this SFF. After you remove the drive rack, you can install all of your drives and then screw the rack back into the case as one unit. Here's what you need to do:

1. Remove the case cover as just described.

2. You'll see two rack mount screws at the top of the case, which secure the drive rack. Using a screwdriver, remove both screws and set them aside (**Figure 10.3**).

Figure 10.3: Using a screwdriver, remove the two screws from the top of the drive rack that attach it to the case.

3. Remove the drive rack by sliding it back and up.

4. Remove the front bay cover by removing the screws on each side of the mounting rack. You will not need the cover anymore, so place it out of the way (**Figure 10.4**).

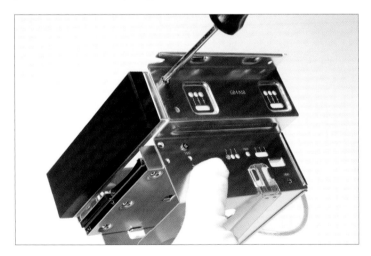

Figure 10.4: Using a screwdriver, remove the four screws that hold the front bay covers to the rack. You no longer need these covers so place them somewhere out of the way.

Sweeet!

Look closely at the ICE module before you take it out. It's not hard to remove, but it's easier to reinstall later if you pay attention to the way it's positioned now.

5. Turn the rack over and look at the plastic cable holder attached to the bottom of the rack—you'll use that later. Right now, we just want you to know that it's there. You'll need to do some more case prep before installing the drives. Go ahead and place the rack to the side for now (**Figure 10.5**).

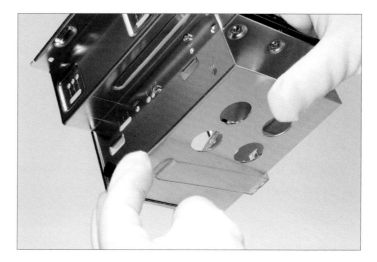

Figure 10.5: Take a look at the cable holder on the bottom of the rack, then set the rack aside; you'll use it later.

How to Remove the ICE Module

Before you can install the processor, you need to get the ICE (Integrated Cooling Engine) module—a compact cooling system—out of your way. Because this case is so cramped for space, a big processor cooler like we use in larger cases simply won't fit. The ICE module, custom built for the Shuttle SFF, has a heat sink that transfers heat to little radiator pipes that then remove the heat from the case via an exhaust fan.

Removing the ICE module isn't difficult—you won't need to use much force to remove or install it.

1. Turn the case over and unscrew and remove the four ICE fan thumbscrews that secure the fan to the back of the case (**Figure 10.6**).

Figure 10.6: Remove the four thumbscrews holding the ICE module to the back of the case.

2. Return the case to its upright position and, reaching in through the side of the case, press down on the retaining clip to release the ICE module heat sink from the socket (**Figure 10.7**).

Figure 10.7: Press down on the retaining clip to release the ICE module heat sink from the socket.

3. Unplug the fan connector located at the bottom of the cooling fan (**Figure 10.8**).

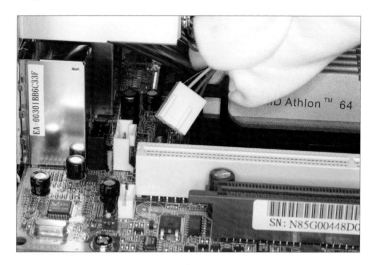

Figure 10.8: Unplug the fan power connector.

4. Using care, pull forward on the radiator that is attached to the back of the case and lift up on the heat sink to remove the ICE module from the case—it should come out as one unit (**Figure 10.9**).

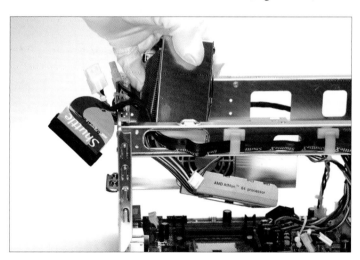

Figure 10.9: Remove the ICE module from the case by carefully bringing the radiator forward and lifting up on the heat sink—the whole unit will come out as one piece.

Installing the Processor

Now that the prep work is out of the way, we'll show you how to put together all of the pieces that make up a Little Dude, starting with the processor. You won't need a motherboard because this SFF has a preinstalled motherboard that's designed specifically for this case. You *will* install a processor, video card, hard drive, optical drive, and memory, however; so if you decide to stray from our design, you'll have plenty of opportunities to customize your PC.

How to Install the Processor

Building a computer isn't brain surgery, although installing a processor is as close as you'll come to it. The processor is, after all, the brains behind your Little Dude's brawn. Use care in handling your processor—it's delicate, expensive, and your computer is useless without it.

1. Pull up the processor socket lever; you don't need any special tools to do this. The socket lever, which is located next to the socket, locks the processor in place. Lifting up the lever unlocks the socket and allows you to remove or insert the processor (**Figure 10.10**).

Figure 10.10: Pull up the processor socket lever to unlock the socket.

Sweeet!

If you want to save money without sacrificing performance, buy an AMD processor. As of this writing, an Intel Pentium 4 2.8 GHz processor costs $160, whereas an AMD Athlon 64 2800+ (AMD's equivalent to the Pentium 4) only costs $125. That's a savings of $35. Plus, the AMD processor is 64-bit, while the Pentium 4 is still a 32-bit processor.

2. Insert the processor in the socket by matching the triangle on the corner of the processor with the triangle in the socket corner (**Figure 10.11**).

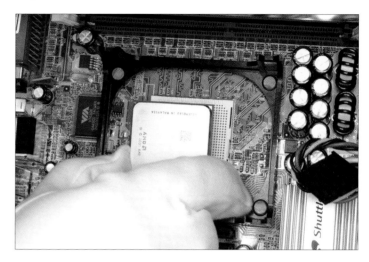

Figure 10.11: Insert the processor in the socket, matching the triangle on the socket to the one on the processor.

3. Push the socket lever down to secure the processor (**Figure 10.12**).

Figure 10.12: Lock the lever, and then place a small dab of thermal compound on the processor.

4. Spread a thin layer of thermal compound on the processor using a plastic card (**Figure10.13**).

Figure 10.13: Spread a thin, even layer of thermal compound on the processor using a card.

5. Replace the ICE module by reversing your earlier steps. Using care, place the heat sink on the processor as you lower the radiator into position in the back of the case (**Figure 10.14**).

Figure 10.14: Replace the ICE module by reversing the removal process.

Sweeet!

Don't forget to push the socket lever down after you insert the processor. You'll damage the processor very quickly if you don't lock it into place.

Sweeet!

Thermal compound does not come with the processor or the Shuttle case, so you'll have to buy some. We use and recommend Arctic Silver. It works well and spreads easily. Remember, you want a very thin layer—don't just slap it on there. Spread it on like a thin layer of butter.

6. Plug in the fan's power connector to the motherboard fan connector located next to the processor socket. Check to make absolutely sure that it's connected (**Figure 10.15**). We can't stress this enough. If the fan is not plugged in, you will fry your processor and ruin your PC.

Figure 10.15: Plug the fan power connector back into the motherboard from where you unplugged it.

7. By reaching through the side of the case, secure the heat sink with the retaining clip that you removed earlier, making sure to attach the solid side first.

8. Insert the hooks into the holes and buckle the other side by pressing the clip down with both hands. This requires some force, but be careful not to overdo it (**Figure 10.16**).

Figure 10.16: Refasten the ICE module heat sink to the socket with the retaining clip.

9. Carefully turn the PC onto its side and screw the smart fan to the case using the four thumbscrews you removed earlier.

10. Two cables will run along the right side of the ICE module after you have installed it—you need to secure these cables to the ICE module. For this, you will use a square piece of adhesive foam tape and a wire tie—both of which are included with the Shuttle case. Neatly stick the tape over the wire tie and secure the wires to the ICE module so that they don't rattle or get in the way (**Figure 10.17**).

 **Sweeet!**

One more time: You must connect your processor fan before you turn on this PC or you will fry your processor. Triple-check all of your fan connections before powering up this system.

Figure 10.17: Secure the two cables running beside the ICE module radiator with a piece of tape and a wire tie.

Installing Memory

OK. Time for a progress check. By now, you should have successfully removed the hard drive rack to gain access to the ICE module, removed the ICE module, installed the processor, and reinstalled the ICE module, which includes plugging in the fan's power cord to the motherboard. It's very important that you double check the fan connection and ensure that the clips tightly secure your ICE module in place. If anything goes wrong with your fan, your processor could overheat, and you'd be out one sweet PC.

Moving on . . . the next thing you need to do is install your memory.

How to Install Memory

RAM (Random Access Memory) is the place where all the work is done. It is temporary storage where the operating system, application programs, and data currently being used are kept so that they can be quickly reached by the computer's processor. Let's go install some.

1. Look through the side of your case and find your DIMM (memory) slots.

2. Unlock the DIMM latches by pulling the tabs outward. Unlocking these latches allows you to insert your memory sticks.

3. Place your memory over top of the DIMM slots and ensure that the alignment notch on the memory stick matches that of the slots. You'll see that there is one row of contacts on the DIMM slot that's shorter than the other—make sure these match up with the connectors on the memory stick. Slide the memory into the DIMM slot smoothly until it is resting on top of the latches.

4. When you're confident that the memory stick is aligned appropriately and in place, push down evenly until the latches close. You'll have to press down with some force to close the latches; just be careful to push down straightly and evenly (**Figure 10.18**).

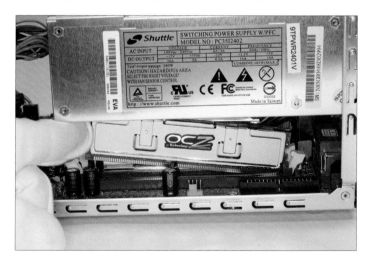

Figure 10.18: Install RAM one at a time, making sure they align with the DIMMs.

5. Visually confirm that the latches are closed and that your memory is firmly installed. The memory is securely installed when the memory stick looks straight and well seated in the DIMM slot and the latches have moved from the outward position to the vertical position. It'll be pretty obvious if the memory isn't seated properly.

6. Repeat steps 1 through 5 with the second memory stick.

 **Sweeet!**

Make sure that your memory matches the DIMM slot notch. You can break the memory or, even worse, damage the DIMM slot by trying to force the memory in the wrong way.

Cables, Drives, and Cards

Processor installed? Check. Memory installed? Check. Now it's time to load up your drives and install your video card. The first step involves connecting a few vital cables. Please pay attention because this is not covered in any of your manuals. Because the Little Dude's case is so small, after you install the drive rack it's impossible to access some important plugs and connections. (The manual neglects to warn you about this.)

The drive rack is arranged so that all of the drives are stacked like pancakes, one on top of the other. This saves space, but it also makes it difficult to keep the components cool—less space for air to circulate—and it makes it hard to work on the drives after the drive rack has been installed.

How to Install the Drive Cables and Drive Rack

Follow along closely—this is the best way we've found to accomplish the next few steps. If you perform the steps out of order, it will take twice the time to remove the cables and drive rack so that you can access some of these connections. Believe us, we have done this before and do not want you to waste time making the same mistake.

Sweeet!

The SATA cables only go in one way, so make sure you line up your connectors correctly.

1. Start by finding the SATA cable—it's that small, thin, blue or red cable that has the small black plug on the end of it. If you look into the end of the plug, you'll see that it has an L-shaped connection point. Plug one end, it doesn't matter which, in to the SATA connection (labeled SATA 1) on the front of the motherboard (**Figure 10.19**).

Figure 10.19: Plug the SATA cable into the SATA slot labeled "SATA 1."

2. In the upper right corner at the back of the case, you'll see a bundle of wires tied together with a white plastic tie called a *purse lock*. Release the purse lock and separate the cables a bit so that you can work with them. When you're finished building the computer, you'll reinstall the purse lock to secure those loose cables to the chassis of the case.

3. If you're using an IDE hard drive, grab it and set the jumper on the back to "master" by placing it on the two pins under MA (**Figure 10.20**). If you're following our recommendations for this build and using an SATA hard drive and motherboard, you don't have to do this. If you decided on an IDE cable system, however, it's much more convenient to set this jumper *before* you install the hard drive, so don't skip this step.

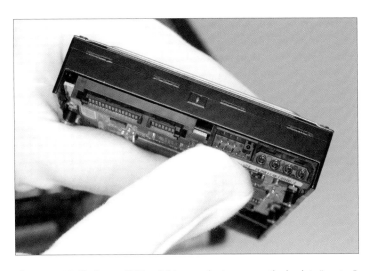

Figure 10.20: If using an IDE hard drive, set the jumper on the back to "master."

4. Slide your hard drive in on the bottom of the drive rack underneath the metal side tabs. You'll need to slide the hard drive in backward, so make sure the connectors at the back of the drive face away from the slots in the top of the rack where it slides into the case (**Figure 10.21**).

 **Sweeet!**

Your hard drive has three sets of pins: CS, which stands for cable select; SL, which stands for slave; and MA, which stands for master. You can use CS if you have only one drive, although we prefer to use MA because it specifically assigns the hard drive as master. We've seen hard drives not function in CS mode. You'd use SL if you had a second hard drive installed in your system for backup or for extra storage space. We used to see a lot of systems with two hard drives, but now it's more cost effective to get a large external Universal Serial Bus (USB) drive instead.

Figure 10.21: Install the hard drive in the rack with the connection slots to the back of the case. Use the four screws provided with the hard drive.

5. Double check that you installed the drive correctly—the front of the hard drive (the front has no connection points) should not extend past the front of the rack.

6. Using the screws that came with your hard drive, screw your hard drive to the rack, installing two screws in each side through the holes in the rack that line up with the holes in the hard drive.

7. After you have the hard drive installed, place the drive rack back in your case through the top and slide it down and forward to reseat it (**Figure 10.22**).

Figure 10.22: Reinstall the rack with the hard drive attached. Secure the rack with the two screws you removed earlier.

8. Screw the drive rack into the case using the two screws you removed earlier from the top of the rack.

9. Route the hard drive's SATA cable underneath the drive rack that you just installed. There is a cable holder attached to bottom of the rack (remember?) that will help you keep all your cables secure and out of the way.

10. Find the SATA power cable that's connected to your power supply, the connection looks like the regular SATA cable connection only larger. Plug in both the SATA data cable and the SATA power cable to the hard drive (**Figure 10.23**).

Figure 10.23: Plug the SATA data cable and SATA power cable into the hard drive.

11. Connect the card reader cable (there is only one cable to connect) to the connection point on the motherboard labeled USB2. The connection point is just to the back of the IDE sockets and has five pins in a protected white socket (**Figure 10.24**).

Figure 10.24: Connect the card reader cable to the plug labeled "USB 2."

Sweeet!

There are three types of power cables that carry power from the power supply to the components. The 4-pin cable is the largest and usually goes to the optical drives (CD and DVD). The SATA power cable, which powers the SATA hard drive, is thin and has an L shape like the SATA data cable. The other type of power cable is smaller and provides power for that high-powered video card. Take a close look at all the power cables leaving the power supply and then examine the backs of your drives to see how all the cables differ.

Congratulations! You've passed the halfway point! If you're just reading through this process, it might seem like a lot of work. In reality, it's not as hard or time consuming as it sounds. (The first time we ever built a Little Dude, it took us about 40 minutes, now we can do it in 15.) All you need to do now is install the DVD burner and your video card before you move into setting up the software.

How to Install the DVD Burner

The DVD burner goes in from the front of the case. By this point, you should be able to see the method to our madness. If you had installed the drives in the rack earlier, you would now have to remove the rack because the screws would have been in the wrong holes or you wouldn't be able to get to the back of the other drives to make the connections. We're here to make your life easy, see?

1. On the DVD burner, set the drive jumper to "master" since this will be the only optical drive you use in this installation (**Figure 10.25**).

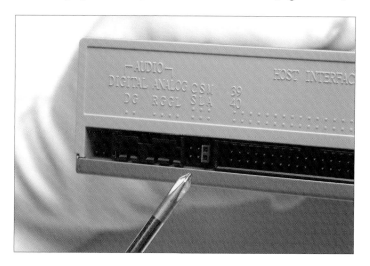

Figure 10.25: On the DVD burner, set the jumper to "master."

2. Slide the DVD burner into the case through the front bay until it is flush with the face of the case.

3. When the drive is in place, the #2 holes in the rack should line up with the screw holes for the drive. You'll be able to see the numbered alignment holes by looking through the sides of the case (**Figure 10.26**).

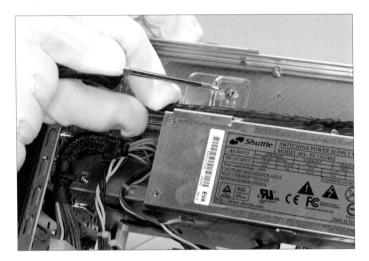

Figure 10.26: Slide the DVD burner in place and secure it with four screws.

4. Find the IDE cable, which came preinstalled and fastened to the case—it should be dangling right next to the back of your drive. Plug this cable into the back of your DVD burner (**Figure 10.27**).

Figure 10.27: Connect the preinstalled IDE cable to the back of the DVD burner.

5. Find the power cable, which will be the large 4-pin type, and plug that into the back of your DVD burner as well (**Figure 10.28**).

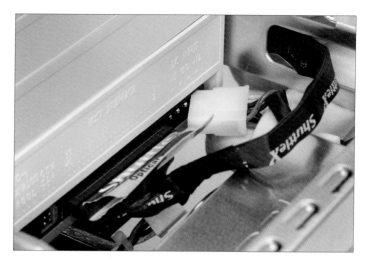

Figure 10.28: Connect a 4-pin power cable to the DVD burner.

6. Ensure that you neatly routed all of your cables to keep your case neat and to allow room for airflow.

How to Install the Video Card

Before you can install the video card, you need to remove the expansion slot covers. Fortunately, Shuttle has made this pretty easy to do.

1. To remove the expansion slot covers, you must first find the two screws that hold the expansion slot bracket in place. You should find them on the outside of the case, behind and above the accelerated graphics port (AGP) slot.

2. Remove both screws and lift up the bracket to remove the slot covers (**Figure 10.29**).

Figure 10.29: Remove the screws in the bracket and remove the slot covers.

3. On the inside of the machine, find the AGP slot, which is the brown slot on the right edge of the motherboard, and push down on the white latch to open it (**Figure 10.30**).

Figure 10.30: Push down on the lock on the AGP slot to unlock the slot for the video card.

Sweeet!

When you first turn on your new PC, check to make sure the fans start up. You can do this when you set up the BIOS (we'll get into that next), but no matter what, do it very shortly after you start the system or you risk frying your new PC if the fan fails for any reason.

4. Place the video card in the AGP slot and pull up on the white latch to secure it (**Figure 10.31**).

Figure 10.31: Install the video card in the AGP slot by aligning it and pressing down on the card. Pull up on the lock to engage it.

5. Find one of the extra 4-pin power connecters coming from the power supply and connect it to the video card (**Figure 10.32**).

Figure 10.32: Connect a 4-pin power supply cable to the video card.

Dude, you just built a Small Form Factor computer! Feels pretty good, doesn't it? We're guessing that you now want to plug it in and get it running, but there are just a few more things you need to take care of first.

1. Triple-check all your power and fan connections and make sure your cables are neatly routed and tucked out of the way.

2. Next, replace the case cover by sliding it down and forward.

3. With the case cover on, turn over the computer and screw in the three thumbscrews that you removed at the beginning of this project.

4. Finally, hook up all your peripherals, including your keyboard, mouse, and monitor. Now, check out your sweet rig (**Figure 10.33**).

Sweeet!

We chose not to install the front feet that come with the case, but if you want to install them, simply screw the feet into the appropriate holes.

Figure 10.33: Pretty sweet, eh?

 **Sweeet!**

Prior to setting up the BIOS, make sure to read the motherboard manual completely.

Setting Up the BIOS

BIOS, which stands for Basic Input/Output System, is the onboard programming that allows your motherboard and components to communicate at the most basic levels. It allows you to configure how everything will work. You'll use the BIOS to configure your controllers and drives and to set the date and time for your PC.

For this installation, we show you how to set up optimized defaults and then we show you a few changes we make to them. If the BIOS looks a little foreign, don't be afraid. Getting around in the BIOS is easier than it seems on the surface. Use the Enter key to select a submenu or item and use the Esc (Escape) key to back out of a menu after you select your changes.

How to Set Up the BIOS

The manual may make this process seem difficult, but it really isn't. You only have to configure a few settings for your system to operate properly. Follow our BIOS guide and you shouldn't have any problems.

1. Power on your Little Dude and immediately press the Delete key repeatedly until you see the Phoenix-Award BIOS CMOS Setup Utility screen.

2. Select "Load Optimized Defaults" and press the Enter key.
   Type "y" when prompted to load the defaults (**Figure 10.34**).

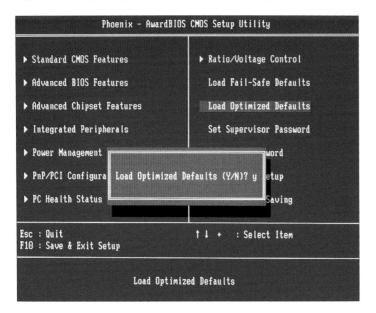

Figure 10.34: Load "Optimized Defaults" as a starting point in the BIOS.

Sweeet!

You can always turn off your system by pressing the power button for about five seconds. You can then reenter the BIOS by pressing the Delete key as the computer powers up. This is a good thing to know for the future—you may need it. When you're navigating the BIOS menu, you use the arrow keys, the Tab key, or the Scroll key to move the highlighted cursor up, down, left, and right. The + (plus) and − (minus) keys allow you to select some settings. To select a menu item, use the Enter key, and to back out of a menu, use the Esc key. These are basic functions and are the same for all the BIOS systems we've used.

3. Select "Standard CMOS Features" and press the Enter key (**Figure 10.35**).

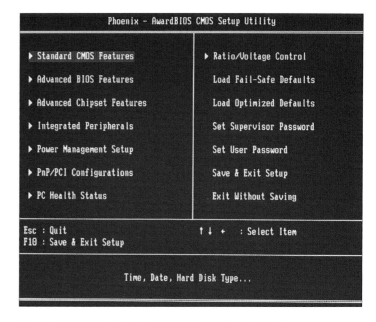

Figure 10.35: Select "Standard CMOS Features" and press Enter.

4. Using the + (plus) and − (minus) keys, set the date and time (**Figure 10.36**).

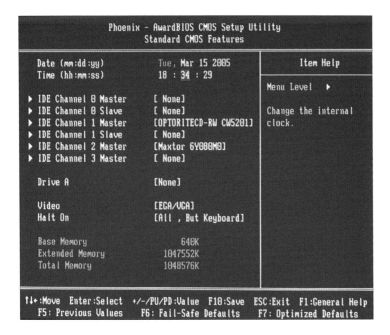

Figure 10.36: Set the time and date using the arrow keys.

5. Hit the Esc key until returned to the Phoenix-Award BIOS CMOS Setup Utility screen—it's the first main screen.

6. Select "Advanced BIOS Features" and press the Enter key.

7. Select "First Boot Device" and press the Enter key (**Figure 10.37**).

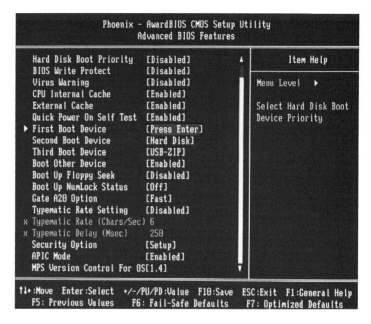

Figure 10.37: Select "First Boot Device" to set boot priority.

8. In the window that opens, select "CD-ROM" and press the Enter key (**Figure 10.38**).

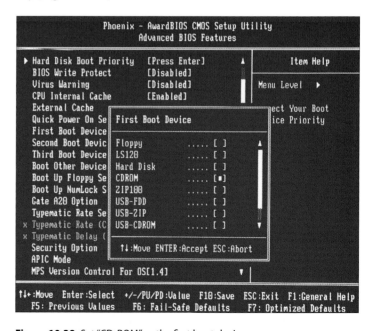

Figure 10.38: Set "CD-ROM" as the first boot device.

9. Select "Integrated Peripherals" and press the Enter key (**Figure 10.39**).

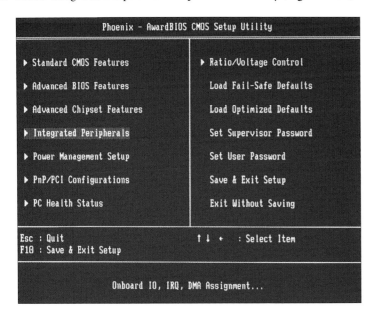

Figure 10.39: Select "Integrated Peripherals" and press Enter.

10. The submenu will have an option for "Onboard PCI Device." Highlight that option and press the Enter key (**Figure 10.40**).

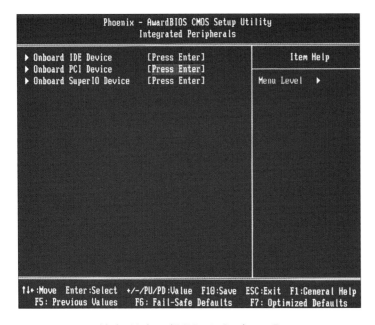

Figure 10.40: Highlight "Onboard PCI Device" and press Enter.

11. Set the "Init Display First" to "AGP Slot" and press Enter (**Figure 10.41**).

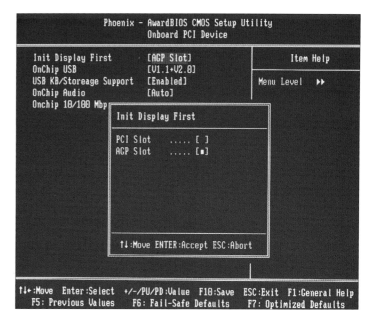

Figure 10.41: Select "AGP Slot" as the "Init Display First" and press Enter.

12. Hit the Esc key until returned to the Phoenix-Award BIOS CMOS Setup Utility screen.

13. Highlight "Save & Exit Setup" and press Enter. In case you selected this option by accident, the BIOS will ask, "Save to CMOS and EXIT Y/N?" Press "Y" to continue. (**Figure 10.42**). That's it! You're done. On to Windows.

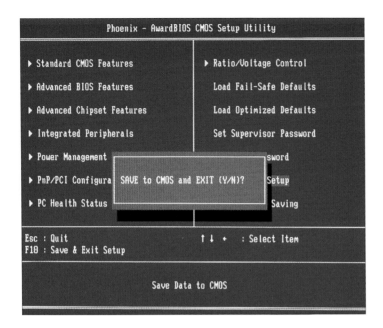

Phoenix - AwardBIOS CMOS Setup Utility

▶ Standard CMOS Features   ▶ Ratio/Voltage Control

▶ Advanced BIOS Features   Load Fail-Safe Defaults

▶ Advanced Chipset Features   Load Optimized Defaults

▶ Integrated Peripherals   Set Supervisor Password

▶ Power Management   sword

▶ PnP/PCI Configura   SAVE to CMOS and EXIT (Y/N)?   Setup

▶ PC Health Status   Saving

Esc : Quit   ↑ ↓ ← : Select Item
F10 : Save & Exit Setup

Save Data to CMOS

Figure 10.42: Select "Save & Exit Setup" and press Enter.

Installing Windows XP Home Edition

The BIOS is nice, but it's no Windows. In order for your computer to operate, it needs an operating system. Windows XP Home Edition is the popular choice for most home PC users. Even without any other software installed, this operating system gives you a basic bundle of applications that allows you to configure an Internet and/or email account, write plain text in Notepad, burn CDs, chat via Windows Messenger, and play music CDs. It even includes a couple of basic games, such as Solitaire and FreeCell.

Installing Windows can be confusing if you don't know what you're doing. If you're unsure of how to configure your settings, your install may seem to take a long time or you may have to reconfigure some items after the install. No need to worry though. We'll show you the best way to configure your operating system to minimize the hassle and to get you losing at Solitaire in no time.

How to Install Windows XP Home Edition

1. Insert the Windows XP Installation CD into your drive.

2. Restart your computer by pressing the reset switch.

3. When your computer restarts, it takes you to the Windows XP Home Edition Setup menu.

4. In the Windows XP Home Edition Setup menu, press Enter to select "To Setup Windows XP now" (**Figure 10.43**).

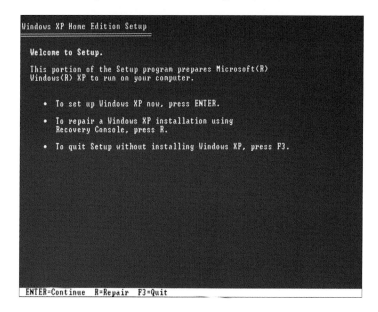

Figure 10.43: Select "To set up Windows XP now" by pressing Enter.

5. Read the Windows XP Licensing Agreement and press the F8 key to continue.

6. Use your up and down arrow keys to select "To set up Windows XP on the selected item, press ENTER" and then press the Enter key (**Figure 10.44**). If this is a brand new hard drive (as is the case for most of you), or if you only have one hard drive installed (which we highly recommend), then you only see one item to select labeled "Unpartitioned Space." In this case, just press the Enter key.

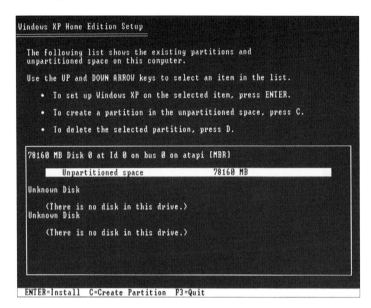

Figure 10.44: Highlight "Unpartitioned Space" and hit Enter to set up Windows on the hard drive.

Sweeet!

We advise that you put that product code sticker on your computer for safe keeping and quick reference because it's the only evidence you have that you bought Windows. That code cost you in the neighborhood of $100, so don't lose it. Microsoft wants you to put it where it can be seen—we usually put it on the back. If you ever need to reload Windows, you'll need this code.

7. Select "Format the partition using the NTFS file system" and press the Enter key (**Figure 10.45**). Don't choose the "Quick" option unless you've formatted your hard drive once before. The first time you format a drive, it should be a regular format.

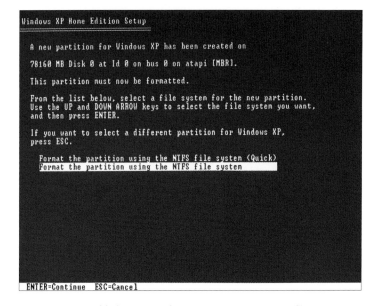

Figure 10.45: Highlight "Format the partition using the NTFS file system" and press Enter.

8. Once your PC is done formatting your hard drive and copying setup files, let it reboot automatically. You could press Enter to restart, but we suggest you wait, just in case Windows is doing something behind the scenes. After a restart, Windows continues with the setup.

9. As Windows loads, it asks you to make some choices. When the Regional and Language Options window appears, click Next, unless you speak something other than English and want to customize the language.

10. In the Personalize Your Software window, type in your name and click Next.

11. In the Product Key window, enter your product key—it's on that colorful sticker that comes on the outside of your Windows disk; you know, the one that has about 200 characters in the code. After you enter this code, which actually only has 25 characters, go ahead and click Next (**Figure 10.46**).

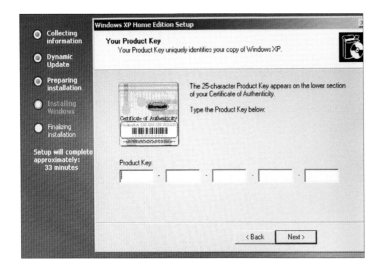

Figure 10.46: Enter the product key and hit Next.

12. In the What's Your Computer's Name? window, type in a name for your computer; it can be anything you want.

13. In the Date and Time Settings window, choose your date, time, and time zone from their respective menus and click Next.

14. In the Network Settings window, click the button next to Typical Settings to select it and click Next.

15. Windows reboots automatically one final time before installation is complete, and upon startup, it takes you to a Welcome screen. Click Next to continue.

16. In the Help Protect Your PC window, select whether or not you would like to activate automatic updates and then click Next. We suggest that you select the automatic updates to stay up-to-date.

17. In the Registration window, you're asked to register your copy of Windows. Chances are you don't have an Internet connection yet, so click "Skip" to skip registration now and register later over the Internet or by phone. Microsoft allows you 30 days to register. Be sure to do it before the 30 days runs out or your machine will stop working and you'll have to start all over again with your Windows installation. To register, all you need is your product key; there isn't a separate registration number.

18. In the Who Will Use This Computer? window, type in the names of all of the people who will use the computer and click Next.

That's it for setting up Windows. Now, let's load some drivers.

Installing Drivers and Software

After you perform the initial setup, Windows should load a clean, empty desktop on your monitor (**Figure 10.47**). This virgin desktop has Windows installed, but you still need to load *drivers*, which basically allow Windows to recognize and communicate with your components.

Figure 10.47: A view of a nice, clean desktop.

How to Install Shuttle Drivers

Installing drivers is similar to installing Windows, they pretty much load themselves with minimal help.

1. Insert the CD that came with your motherboard. It should play automatically.

2. From the Mainboard Software Setup window, click "Install Mainboard Software" (**Figure 10.48**).

Figure 10.48: Select the "Install Mainboard Software" option.

3. Without changing any of the default settings, click "Install INVIDIA Chipset Drivers" and load all the drivers.

4. After they're all loaded, exit the Driver window, which takes you back to the Mainboard Software Setup menu, and click "Quit."

How to Install Video Card Drivers

This one is just like the last one, put the disk in and let 'er rip.

1. Insert the ATI Radeon Driver CD that came with your video card. It should play automatically.

2. From the main setup screen, choose "Display Adapter Driver Setup" (**Figure 10.49**).

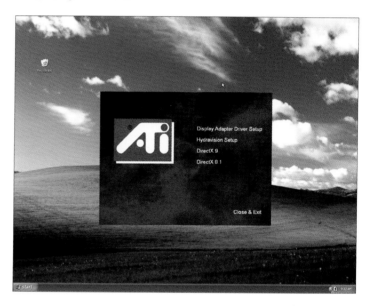

Figure 10.49: Select "Display Adapter Driver Setup" and press Enter.

3. From the submenu, select "ATI Easy Install."

4. When prompted, select "Express Install" and let it load all the drivers.

5. Restart Windows XP when directed.

Dude, you're done! Quit reading this book and go enjoy your new computer!

Chapter 11

Basic Troubleshooting

Congratulations, you did it! You built your very own PC from the ground up.

What?

You say the computer won't turn on? The sound won't work?

Don't worry. We've pulled together a few of our top troubleshooting tips to help you solve the most common problems we encounter when building PCs. If you used high quality parts in your build, such as the ones we recommend in these chapters, you shouldn't run into many (if any) problems. In our years of experience building computers, we've found that most problems come from settling for cheaper components.

If you do run into a problem not covered in this chapter, check your motherboard manual, which often has very helpful troubleshooting tips specific to the parts you're using for your machine.

My computer won't turn on.

1. Check the obvious first! Look to make sure you connected the power cable to the back of your power supply and to your electrical outlet.

2. If that doesn't fix the problem, check to ensure that you plugged the power supply's 24-pin power plug into the motherboard.

3. If you still don't get any juice, you either have a bad power supply or a bad motherboard. Return both items and try again when they come in.

My keyboard won't work. Or maybe it's my mouse that's busted?

1. Make sure the keyboard and mouse are plugged into their corresponding ports in the back of your PC.

2. If they are, restart your computer. It's possible that you plugged these in after you booted up your PC—you must turn the computer completely off when you hook up these devices.

3. If you have a Universal Serial Bus (USB) keyboard or mouse, make sure you have USB keyboard and/or mouse support enabled in the BIOS. Remember, to enter the BIOS, you must restart the computer and hit the Delete key immediately and repeatedly as your computer boots up. After you call up the BIOS, work through the screens until you find the Enable setting for USB input devices. More often than not, you can enable USB support for keyboards and mice in the Advanced section of most BIOS programs.

My computer turns on, but nothing happens on the screen.

1. Remove your memory and video card and reinstall them both. These items may not be seated properly or may be making poor contact.

2. Are all of your cables plugged in and secure? Check that your monitor's video connection is plugged into your video card and that its power cable is securely plugged into your electrical outlet.

3. If this doesn't correct the problem, you either have bad memory or a bad video card. If you have another machine lying around that takes your type of memory or video card, try tossing those suckers in to see if they work. Otherwise, you'll need to send back the memory *and* the video card because there's no good way to determine which one failed.

I get a Non-System Disk Error when I try to boot up.

- Remove the floppy disk from your floppy drive. This is a common error made by even the most seasoned veterans, so don't sweat it, it's no big deal.

My sound doesn't work. Seriously, I can't hear a thing.

1. Make sure that your speakers are connected to the output jack in the back of your PC. Check the color of the jack—if you have a single wire, it should be plugged into the green jack.

2. Check to make sure you plugged your power cable into the back of the speakers.

3. If none of this works, uninstall your sound card drivers and then reinstall them. It's possible that you forgot to install them in the first place.

4. If reinstalling the drivers doesn't work, you either have a bad sound card or the sound card isn't compatible with your system. Either way, return the sound card and get a new one, but make sure the new one is high quality and compatible with your system.

My PC boots up, but then it starts beeping and doesn't get past the first screen.

1. Typically, motherboard manufacturers incorporate a combination of long and short beeps as error codes in their motherboards to help users troubleshoot. If there is something wrong with your PC, the motherboard should provide you with a series of beeps. To diagnose what is wrong with your system, match the pattern of beeps coming from your motherboard to one of the patterns described in your motherboard manual.

Instead of using beep patterns, some motherboards now come with a small two-number display that lights up when there is a problem. You can look up this number in your motherboard manual to find out what's going wrong. This number system has begun to replace the beep codes as the new standard for trouble-shooting.

2. If you can't find an explanation in your manual, carefully check all of your BIOS settings. It's likely you set up something wrong somewhere in the process.

Windows freezes up on installation.

1. Start your Windows installation all over again. This doesn't occur often, but it has happened to us a couple of times. Sometimes the CD skips and, as a result, your hard drive may not load all the necessary setup files.

2. If reinstalling Windows doesn't help, you probably have a bad hard drive. Remove your hard drive, return it, and get a new one.

Index

DVD drives. *See also* optical drives
    Gamer PC, 60
    installing, 111–113
    overview, 34–35
    recommendations, 34–35
DVD players, 50, 65
DVDs, 34–35, 60, 68, 88
DVI connectors, 61

E

ECC (Error Correcting Code) memory, 15–16
EPoX motherboards, 21, 66
Error Correcting Code (ECC) memory, 15–16
errors, 177. *See also* troubleshooting
Ethernet cards, 36
expansion slot covers, 156–158
expansion slots, 156–158

F

fan assembly, 100
fan connections
    Gamer PC, 99–100, 104, 107–108
    Little Dude PC, 145–146
fan controllers
    Gamer PC, 100, 107–108
    Ultimate Dude PC, 76
fan power, 104, 142, 146
fans, 37–39. *See also* cooling solutions
    aftermarket, 37–39
    case, 38–39
    noise, 26, 39
    processor, 23, 147
    video cards and, 23
flash drives, 79
flat panel display, 78
flat panel monitors, 51, 53, 61, 70
floppy disks, 125
floppy drives
    Gamer PC, 60, 109–111
    Home Office PC, 50
    installing, 112–115
    Multimedia PC, 69
    overview, 32–33
    Ultimate Dude PC, 79
form factor, 20
full-tower case, 21–22

G

Gamer PC, 91–134
    case for, 59, 93–96
    components, 57–62, 92
    cost of, 56
    hard drives, 60, 109–111
    installing bundled software, 131–134
    installing drivers, 131–134
    installing fan controller, 107–108
    installing hard drive, 109–111
    installing motherboard, 102–104
    installing optical drives, 111–116
    installing sound cards, 106–107
    installing video cards, 105–106
    installing Windows XP, 124–130
    memory, 59
    monitor, 60–61
    operating system software, 61, 124–130
    overview, 55–57
    photo of, 7, 56
    power supplies, 59
    preparing case, 93–96
    preparing for assembly, 92–102
    preparing motherboard, 96–102
    processor, 58
    setting up BIOS, 117–123
    sound cards, 60–61, 106–107
    video cards, 59–60, 105–106
gaming. *See also* Gamer PC; Ultimate Dude PC
    memory cache and, 58
    processor coolers and, 37
    resolution and, 60
    SFFs and, 87
    video cards and, 28–30
Gateway PC, 4–5
GeIL memory, 28
Gigabyte motherboards, 21
GPU (graphics processing units), 29–30

H

hard drive cages, 94, 109, 111, 150–151
hard drives
    external, 34
    Gamer PC, 60, 109–111
    Home Office PC, 50
    IDE, 20, 150
    installing, 109–111
    Internet Surfer PC, 53

S

Sapphire video cards, 30
SATA (Serial ATA), 20
SATA cables, 20, 110–111, 150, 152–154
SATA connections, 14
SATA controllers, 20, 71
SATA drivers, 125
SATA hard drives, 20, 34, 68, 71, 110, 150–154
satellite connections, 61, 69, 80
Scott, Dave, 7
screen. *See also* monitors
    blank, 176–177
    resolution, 78
    size, 51, 53, 61
screw anchors, 103
Seagate hard drives, 34, 68
Serial ATA. *See* SATA
SFF (Small Form Factor), 21
SFF cases, 23–24
SFF PC, 23–24, 87. *See also* Little Dude PC
Shuttle cases, 24, 84, 86–87. *See also* Little Dude PC
shuttle drivers, 173
slave drive, 111, 151, 154
Small Form Factor. *See* SFF
socket lever, 143–145
socket retention screws, 96–97
socket types, 15
sockets, 14–16
sound. *See also* audio
    beep sounds, 177–178
    crackling, 31
    hissing, 31
    PC noise, 17, 26, 39, 80, 88, 107
    problems with, 31, 177
    quality of, 31–32
Sound Blaster sound cards, 31- 32, 50, 60–61, 69, 80
sound cards
    cost of, 31–32
    drivers, 134, 177
    Gamer PC, 60–61, 106–107
    Home Office PC, 50
    installing, 106–107
    Little Dude PC, 88
    Multimedia PC, 69
    overview, 17–18, 31–32
    recommendations for, 31–32
    speakers and, 32

Ultimate Dude PC, 80
sound chips, 17–18. *See also* sound cards
speakers
    Gamer PC, 61–62
    Home Office PC, 52
    Little Dude PC, 88, 90
    Multimedia PC, 70–71
    power output, 81
    sound cards and, 32
    Ultimate Dude PC, 82
startup problems, 176–178
static electricity, 92, 97
stock coolers, 37–38
storage, 32–35. *See also* drives
subwoofer, 70

T

tech support, 7, 44, 51
thermal compound, 39, 99, 145
thermal tape, 99
Thermaltake coolers, 37, 39, 74–76, 99
Thermaltake Polo 735, 39, 75, 97, 107–108
tomshardware.com site, 16
Toshiba DVD-ROM drive, 68
tower cases. *See* cases, computer
troubleshooting, 175–178
    beep sounds, 177–178
    blank screen, 176–177
    freezes, 178
    hard drive problems, 178
    keyboard problems, 176
    motherboards, 176–178
    Non-System Disk Error, 177
    sound problems, 31, 177
    startup problems, 176–178
    Windows installations, 125, 178
TV tuners, 30, 67

U

Ultimate Dude PC, 73–82
    case for, 77
    components, 75–82
    cost of, 73
    hard drive, 78–79
    memory, 78

Peachpit
Essential books for the creative community

Visit Peachpit on the Web at www.peachpit.com

- Read the latest articles and download timesaving tipsheets from best-selling authors such as Scott Kelby, Robin Williams, Lynda Weinman, Ted Landau, and more!

- Join the Peachpit Club and save 25% off all your online purchases at peachpit.com every time you shop—plus enjoy free UPS ground shipping within the United States.

- Search through our entire collection of new and upcoming titles by author, ISBN, title, or topic. There's no easier way to find just the book you need.

- Sign up for newsletters offering special Peachpit savings and new book announcements so you're always the first to know about our newest books and killer deals.

- Did you know that Peachpit also publishes books by Apple, New Riders, Adobe Press, Macromedia Press, palmOne Press, and TechTV press? Swing by the Peachpit family section of the site and learn about all our partners and series.

- Got a great idea for a book? Check out our About section to find out how to submit a proposal. You could write our next best-seller!

You'll find all this and more at www.peachpit.com. Stop by and take a look today!

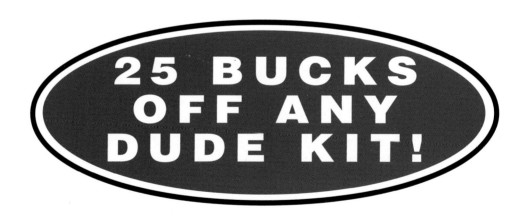